Robert A. Sobieszek   Joan Pedzich   Philip L. Condax   International Museum of Photography at George Eastman House 1984

International Museum of Photography at George Eastman House

Exhibition at International Museum of Photography at George Eastman House April 27–November 30, 1984.
ISBN # 0-935398-10-4

Library of Congress Catalogue Card Number 84:060656

This exhibition is funded in part with a grant from Rochester Sesquicentennial, Inc.

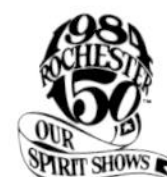

Front Cover: John E. Dumont, The Columbus Fleet Entering Charlotte enroute to Columbia Exposition, 1893.

Flyleaf: Basil Hall, The Village of Rochester, From: Forty Etchings from Sketches Made with the Camera Lucida in North America, Edinburgh, 1829.

International Museum of Photography at George Eastman House 900 East Avenue Rochester, New York 14607

Design: Robert Meyer Design, Inc.

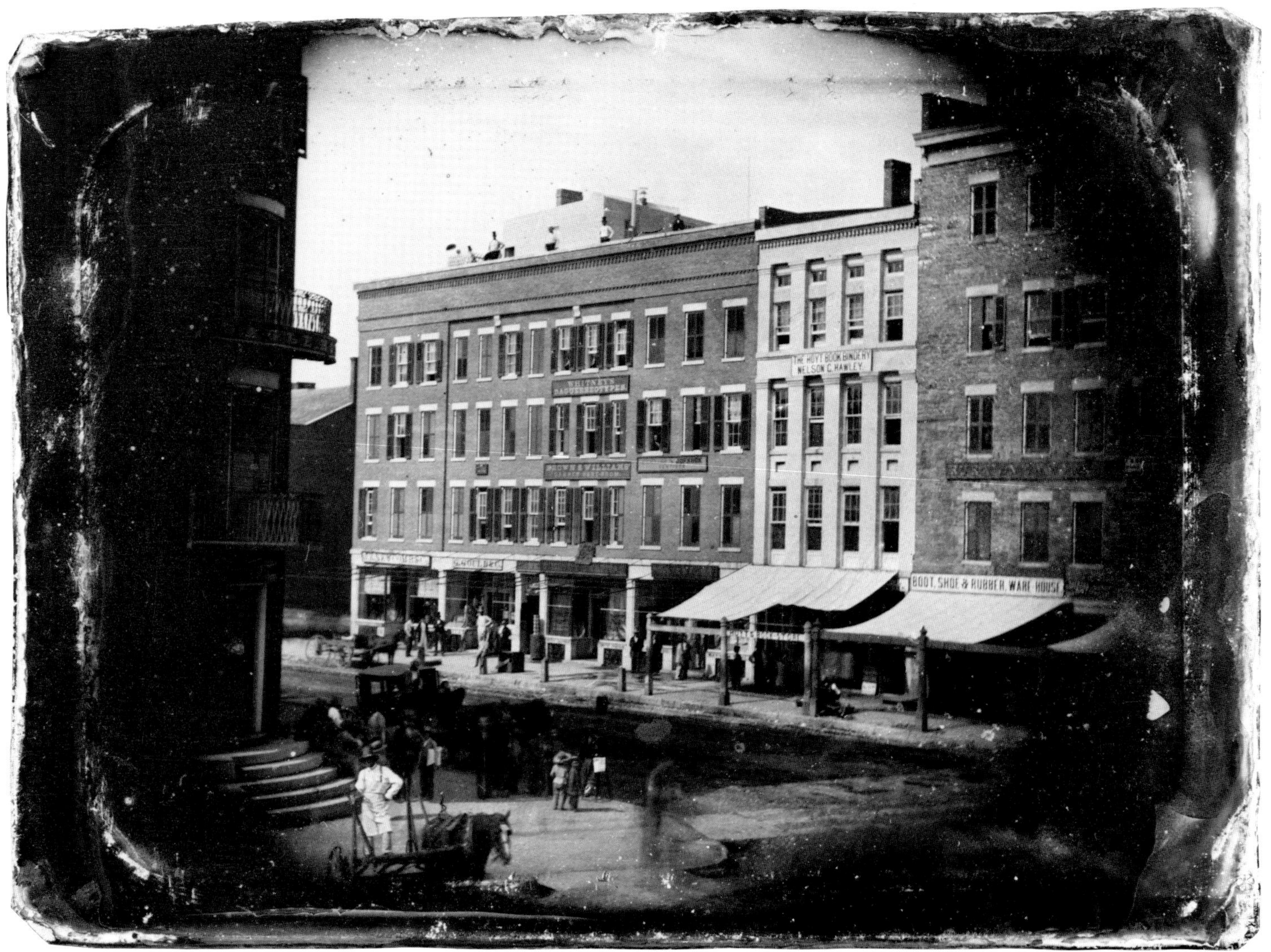

ROCHESTER AND PHOTOGRAPHY

That Rochester may be a unique and pleasant metropolis in Western New York State may not come as too great a surprise to its residents and many of its tourists. That this same city could be called a capital of photography, however, may seem overly chauvinistic and perhaps even a bit patronizing. Yet, if one surveys the history of Rochester through its photographs, and if one studies the history of photography in this city, it is clear that something quite special has been happening for more than the sesquicentennial number of years this city has been around officially. For Rochester has been host and home to a long tradition of photographic achievement—an achievement which has been far more than merely local.

Rochester has been a center of technological innovation, a locus of photographic education, and a cynosure of creative expression within the medium. The list of nationally and internationally known photographers who have lived and worked in Rochester is, with all modesty, long and impressive. It is to them, as well as to two extraordinary visitors whose documentation of the city has been exceptionally seminal, that this exhibition is devoted. And while the focus has been on Rochester photography, it has not been possible to avoid chronicling how the city looked to the various photographic artists who in turn documented, interpreted and expressed the city in which they lived.

THE FIRST VISITOR

Prior to the invention of photography as we know it, photographic history played a decisive role in Rochester. While the city was little more than a small village along the expanding American frontier, Captain Basil Hall of the British Navy interrupted his travels in 1827 so as to render Rochester's few major buildings. Hall used one of the many pre-photographic mechanical devices designed to aid the amateur in correctly delineating a scene, in this case the camera lucida. Although the optics and physics of the camera lucida were unrelated to photography, its use in obtaining a "realistic" picture and in capturing sights by tourists predicted the modern camera. Hall's view of "The Village of Rochester" was included in his **Forty Etchings from Sketches Made with the Camera Lucida in North America,** published in Edinburgh in 1829, a decade before photography. It was with this etching that Rochester began its involvement with photographic history, a history that from the very beginning was international.

THE EARLY YEARS

From the first, and throughout the last century, every process, every technique and nearly every style of photography available in those years was practiced, and practiced well, in the "Flour City." Rochester's very first daguerreian studio opened in 1842, only three years after L. J. M. Daguerre and France gave photography to the world. Little is known of its photographer, Thomas Mercer, and none of his daguerreotypes are in the Museum's collection. We do know, however, that for a while Mercer was a partner with Edward T. Whitney, the city's premier daguerreian artist, and one of the earliest Rochester photographers to gain national prominence for his masterful views of the city and his faultlessly composed and telling portraits, such as his group sitting of the Henry Rochester family. In terms of excellence, Whitney was quickly followed by Richard B. Appleby, whose creative anticipations of college yearbook photography during the 1850s were seemingly unique. Appleby arranged his individual student portraits within impressively substantial hardwood frames labeled as to the year of the graduating class, beginning with the University of Rochester's second commencement in 1854. Although only four of his class portraits have survived, dating from 1854 to 1859, they reveal Appleby as a perfect model of the 19th century professional who was constantly attentive to the fast changing technology of photography. While the "Class of 1854" is comprised of daguerreotypes, the later three classes are rendered either in ambrotype, tintype or a combination of both, all with equal success technically and artistically.

Rochester was, for the most part, not unlike other medium-sized American cities during the last century: proud of a number of innovators and still more certain of a larger number of skilled and talented studio photographers and a host of amateur camera artists who are unsung or even unidentifiable today. Their reliable and straightforward recording of the scenes, events and people of Rochester constitutes a good part of the city's visual history. Thanks to the broad cultural need to picture nearly everything, a need which developed in earnest during the 1860s, Rochester was well documented. And because of such popular photographic formats as the carte-de-visite, the cabinet card, and the stereograph, Rochesterians were well able to collect these images. Photographers like Benjamin Powelson, George Godfrey and Charles Pomeroy, while clearly not among the giants of 19th century artistic photography, adopted the stylistic conventions which adhered to 19th century studio portraiture with perfect taste and facility of means. Landscape stereographers like Myron and George Monroe, Webster and Albee, and publisher Charles Woodward furnished quaint narratives and absolutely stunning views of the city—its great Victorian architecture, its urban and residential street scenes, and its central and perennial symbol, the Genesee River—to a highly enthusiastic audience.

THE LATER CENTURY

Photographically, Rochester went decidedly international by the end of the century on two fronts, one artistic and the other industrial. The most popular and long-lived portrait studio here in the 19th century was that of John Howe Kent. Originally established in Brockport, Kent's studio was exceptionally active for more than four decades, during which this artist was to Rochester what Nadar was to Paris, Hanfstaengl to Munich, and Gutekunst to Philadelphia. Like Appleby before him, Kent adapted a variety of processes, techniques, and formats to his portraiture. In 1876, at the Philadelphia Centennial Exposition, Kent's life-size, or nearly so, portraits were seen by a national and international public, and commentaries about them entered the national press. The Museum is proud to display its three-quarter life-size portrait of an unidentified woman, which would appear to be similar to those exhibited in 1876.

In the arts, the Rochester area has long been recognized as an active center of craft production ever since the late 19th century. At least one Rochester photographer's work, that of John E. Dumont, aligned an American Arts and Crafts sensibility with photography. Little precise information is available about Dumont's life, but it is certain that his proto-pictorialist genre scenes and landscapes won him acclaim in this country, as well as in Europe and India. Dumont saw his photography as essentially the same as painting, that is, a purely pictorial art; and his print, Listening to the Birds, is as fine an artistic gravure as any produced elsewhere. Its delicate tones are reminiscent of those found in the work of Peter Henry Emerson and James Leon Williams in Great Britain; its theme is one that was a favorite of pictorial photographers ever since H. P. Robinson's Hark, Hark, the Lark of 1882, and its device of breaking the image's frame was popular with many artists in the late century.

A UNIVERSAL SYSTEM

Much of Rochester's prestige and world status as a photographic center, of course, is owed to the vision and entrepreneurial industry of a Rochester bank clerk turned photographer. Impatient with the cumbersome and difficult process of the ambrotype, which he learned from stereographer George Monroe in 1877, George Eastman turned toward developing an easier and more universally accessible way of capturing photographic images. To this end, he perfected the manufacturing and marketing of dry plates in 1879, and during the next decade created a full system of flexible roll film, portable camera, and factory processing of film and prints. By 1888, an amateur photographer did not have to bother with chemicals, darkroom, or laborious, heavy equipment; the amateur's involvement with photography was direct, automatic, and summed up by Eastman's slogan: ''You push the button, we do the rest.'' The name Kodak and Eastman's system of perfectly convenient and nearly foolproof photography entered world consciousness well before the turn of the century.

The effects of Eastman's system of photography have been and still remain immeasurable and ubiquitous. Nowhere was Eastman's personal impact on photography more apparent, however, than in the thousands of anonymous snapshots of the period between the late 1880s to the mid-1920s, after which Eastman's direct involvement with his company gradually waned. During this time, Eastman Kodak Company's industrialization, its marketing and advertising, and its devotion to amateur photography transformed the medium from a rather arcane and troublesome blend of chemistry, physics and art into a system of visual language and communication available to most of the world.

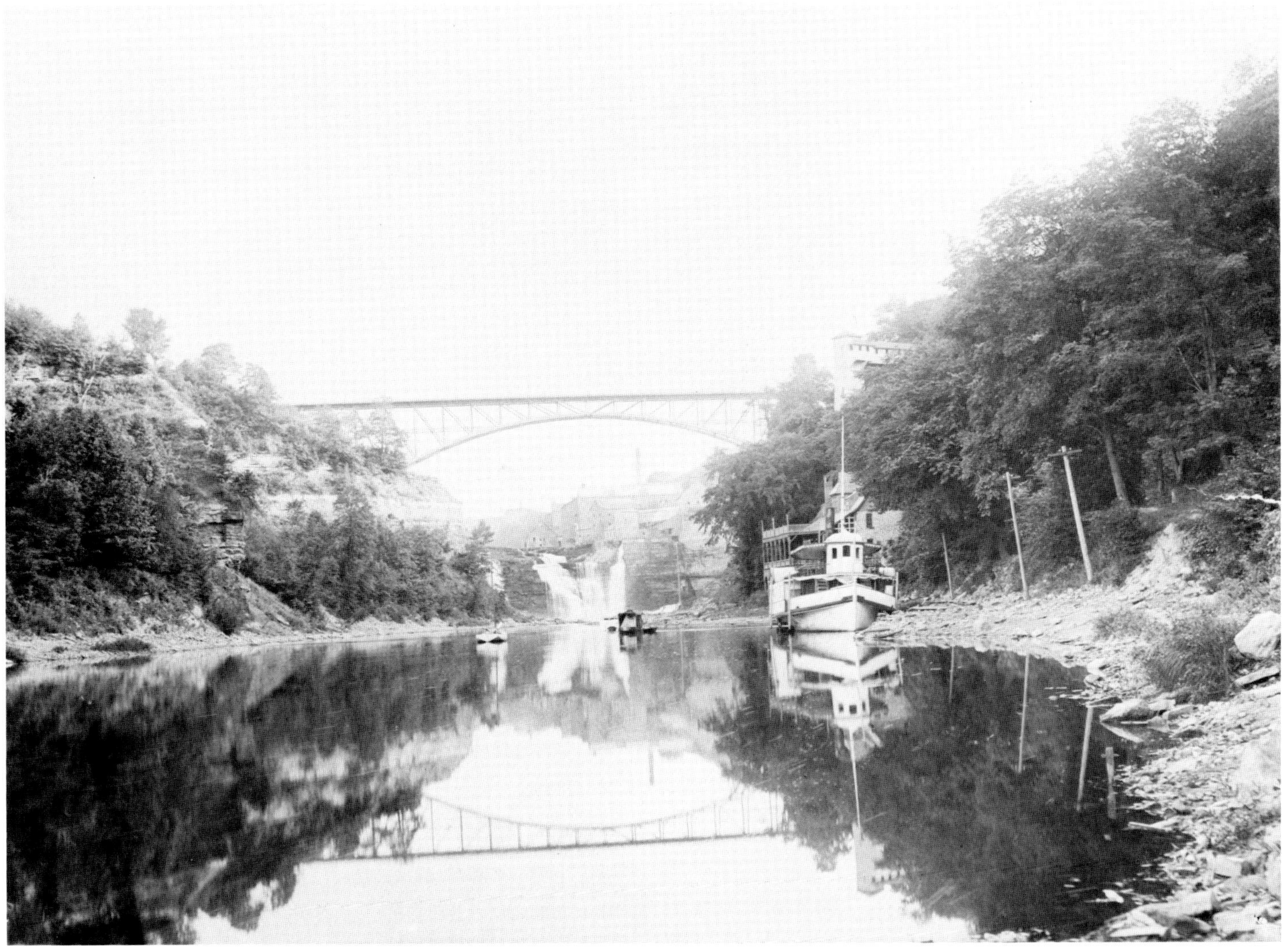

Rochester photography during the early part of this century, like photography in other parts of the country, was marked by new forms brought about in part by new technologies and new processes that allowed for more modern expressions. Photographers had a growing arsenal of cameras, printing techniques, films and papers, as well as a much broader range of aesthetic options opened to them. An artist like Frederick Brehm could apply his engineering training to the invention of a new kind of panoramic camera, the Cirkut, and his poetic sensibility towards creating some of the most spectacular panoramic cityscapes, employee portraits and group portraits of cows ever made. The formal pictorialism that was suggested by Dumont during the last decade of the 19th century reached its fullest expression in such works as Frederick Moser's series of studio portraits of members of the Denio Civic Ballet, or Alexander Leventon's haunting and sensitive portraits of musicians at the Eastman School of Music or other pictorialist photographers whom he knew, such as the famous Czech photographer Frantisek Drtikol.

Glenn Matthews's striking night rendering of a pavilion at the Rochester Centennial Exposition, while still a part of the pictorialist tradition, is fully expressive of a modernist drama and theatricality and, in spirit, similar to other period prints depicting the Chicago Century of Progress in 1934 or the New York World's Fair of 1939. 1934, of course, marked the centenary of Rochester; it was also the year that a Rochester photographer/ technician, Arthur W. Fuchs, made the first full-sized radiographic depiction of a human body on a single sheet of x-ray film. A new form of portraiture in a way, Fuchs's prints may be considered as modernist parallels to John Howe Kent's life-size portraits of the previous century, as well as an important scientific advancement.

Since the beginning of photography, color has been an important factor, leading many photographers to apply paint or pigments to their monochromatic prints. While neither America nor Rochester can lay claim to inventing actual color photography—that credit belongs to other countries, mainly France— Rochester has been more active than any other American city in the development of color photography. Rochesterian Charles Zoller, one of the first Americans to bring the Lumière autochrome to this country, used this early form of in-camera color extensively in and around the city and across the country. An Eastman Kodak Company engineer, John George Capstaff, was instrumental in inventing a different type of glass-plate color photography circa 1915; called Kodachrome, it was a basic two-color process that, in spite of its allure and beauty, did not prove commercially viable. The first truly popular and successful form of color photography had to wait until 1935-36, when Leopold Godowsky, Jr. and Leopold Mannes invented modern Kodachrome film while working with Eastman Kodak Company. Two years later, in 1938, Louis Condax, who was to become a prominent figure in Rochester the following decade, developed what has proven to be one of the most durable and most successful color printing techniques, Kodak Dye Transfer.

Rochester has been a national center for photographers during the last half century. Either they came here to meet with representatives of various companies for technical advice, or, as has been the case since the 1930s, to study, lecture, or participate in programs and exhibitions at any of Rochester's numerous educational institutions. Obviously, the city and its environs have been subjects of a great many photographs made by countless travelers and visitors, professionals and amateurs, students and teachers; far too many to even list, let alone select from and exhibit. Thus, the limits of this exhibition have precluded the work of these visitors and those who resided here as students. Two exceptions, however, have been made: the first was Captain Basil Hall, mentioned above, and the second, one of the most renowned American photograhers of this century, Ansel Adams.

In 1952, the University of Rochester was undergoing a series of expansions and a program of fund raising. The University's Director of Development at the time, Andrew Wolfe, invited Adams to Rochester at the suggestion of Beaumont Newhall, then curator at this Museum. To document the school and the surrounding city, Adams spent a total of six weeks here in the Autumn of that year and produced some of the most eloquent and absolutely masterful photographs of Rochester. His view of downtown Rochester has an operatic grandeur about it that is seldom encountered, in photographs or in reality. As a counterpart to Basil Hall's etching of 1827, Adams's photograph, taken 125 years later, is both a testimony to Rochester's growth and success and an

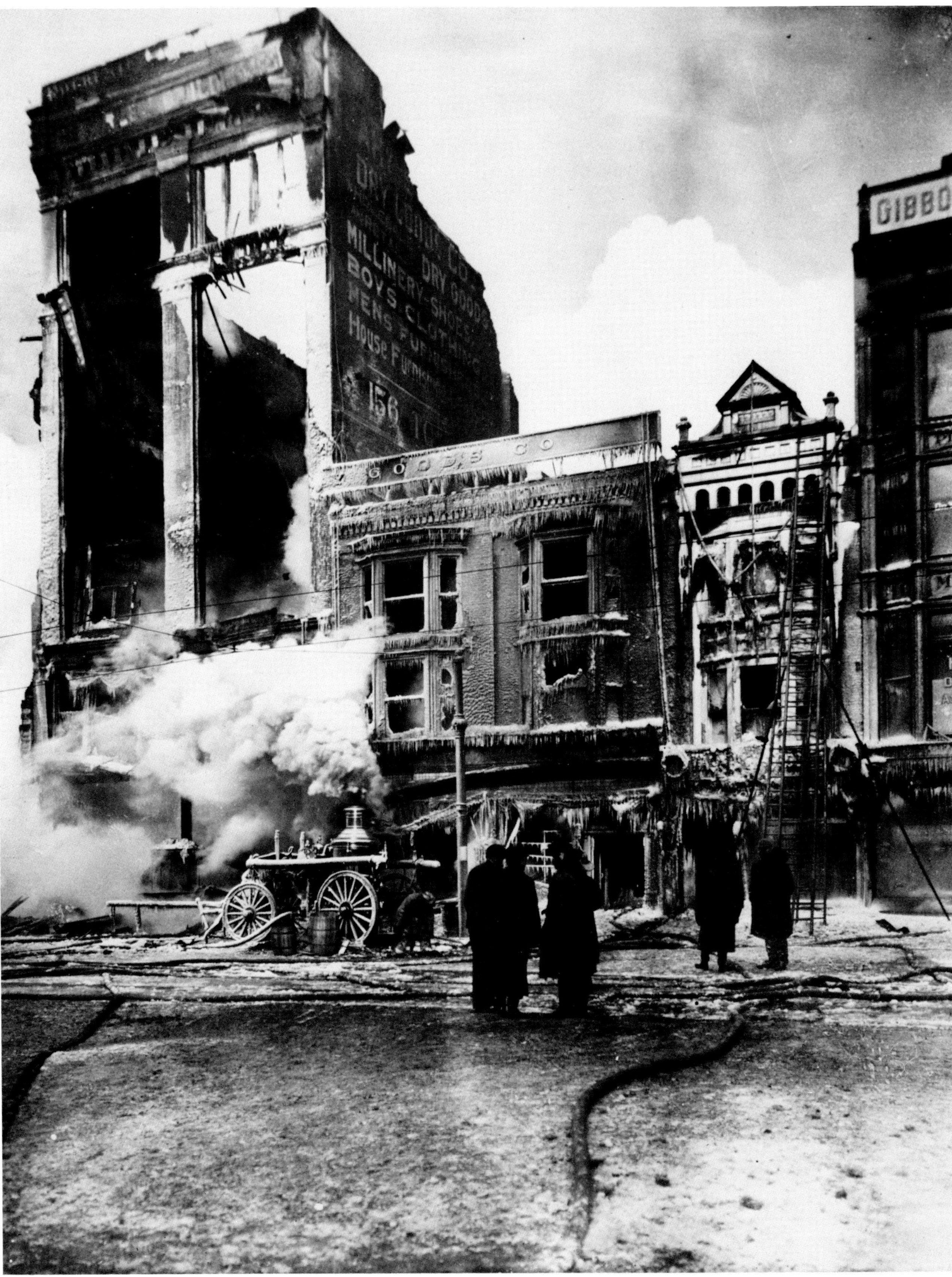

DRY GOODS
MILLINERY · SHOES
BOYS CLOTHING
MENS CLOTHING
House Furni...
156
GOODS CO
GIBBO

affirmation of the progress and achievement of artists using mechanical devices, in this case a camera, as aids to picture making.

THE ERA OF PHOTO-GRAPHIC EDUCATION

Ever since George Monroe taught the ambrotype process to George Eastman in 1877, photographic education has been an active force in Rochester. Charles Zoller lectured widely, using color slides that he made. During World War I, the U.S.A. School of Aerial Photography trained many in the complexities of that skill; and in 1930, the School of Photography at the Rochester Athenaeum and Mechanics Institute was founded at the request of area industry. RAMI's limited technical program was enlarged in 1936 to include also a program of practical photography, such as portraiture, illustration and color. In 1944, RAMI became today's Rochester Institute of Technology, with its photography department housed in the Clark Building at the corner of Broad and Washington Streets. From the initial visions of Frederick Brehm, C. B. Neblette and Mark Ellingson, RIT and its School of Photographic Arts and Sciences has grown to be one of the country's largest and most respected schools of professional technological education.

It was in 1953, however, with the arrival of Minor White in Rochester, that local photographic education greatly expanded its domain of influence. What had been previously devoted almost exclusively to the craft and science of the medium began to address the broader, humanistic issues of photography, such as its art, its sociology and its history. White, one of the key photographic art educators and artists of this century, began as Exhibitions Organizer and Editor at this Museum; in 1955 he joined the faculty at RIT where he and Ralph Hattersly developed the B.F.A. program, first offered at that school in 1960. Following White, Nathan Lyons, again with this Museum as an initial focal point, began a graduate program in photographic art and history in conjunction with SUNY Buffalo in 1968. This program, officially lasting until 1983, became, of course, the Visual Studies Workshop, one of the foremost photographic education centers in the country. The photographic artists of national and even international recognition who have taught at these schools and others, such as the University of Rochester, Nazareth College, and SUNY Brockport, constitute a directory to the various creative attitudes, styles, and voices of contemporary photography. And the work these faculty have produced while here in Rochester represents a very impressive overview of modern artistic and philosophic concerns in the medium.

Educationally, mention must also be made of one of this city's most important and unique resources, the International Museum of Photography at George Eastman House. From its opening in 1949 to the present, "Eastman House" has functioned as America's most active museum devoted exclusively to the art, science and technology of photography and film, attracting, over the years, numberless tourists, scholars, photographers and historians to Rochester. This Museum was not the first such institution in America —that honor belongs to the American Museum of Photograhy, founded in Philadelphia in 1939 and whose collection is now part of our archives and library—but it has certainly amassed the largest and most comprehensive collection of international photography, equipment and cinema, both historical and contemporary, ever assembled. Its reputation has extended far beyond national borders, as have the reputations of its directors, most notably Beaumont Newhall, the dean of American photographic historians.

The modern period of photography in Rochester has been especially fecund and exciting. Since the 1960s, the "Flower City" has been a center of both lilacs and avant-gardism in photographic art. From Walter Chappell's spiritual poetics of the photographic image and Les Krims's provocative gestures of absurd theatrics to Joan Lyons's and Keith Smith's spectacular confrontations of self through unexpected or experimental techniques, photography in Rochester has been consistently refreshed and its expectations defied. At the same time, such High Art photography has coexisted quite comfortably with more traditional forms of camera expression, as seen in the flourishing spheres of advertising, architectural, fashion and portrait photography. Whatever the expression or style, moreover, whether it is a light reflection across a wall on Union Street or a portrait of a chairman of the board, whether it is a view of farm equipment in West Henrietta or farmlands seen from an aircraft, and whether it is a shot recording a gown of black cashmere or one depicting the First Federal Building at night, the subject is still Rochester, a city and its people revealed by the art of the camera.

*Robert A. Sobieszek
Director, Photographic Collections*

*Joan Pedzich
Chief Archivist*

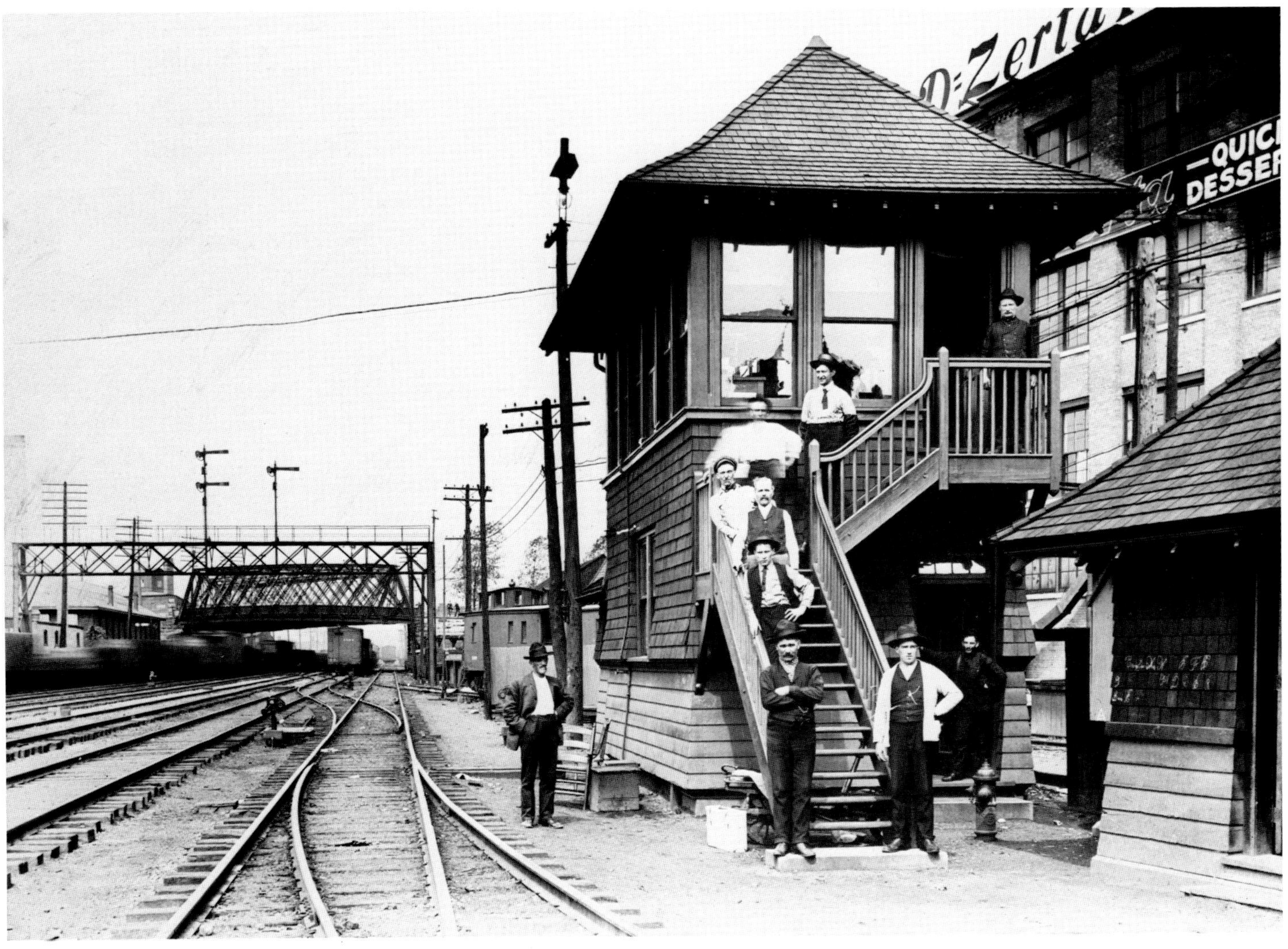

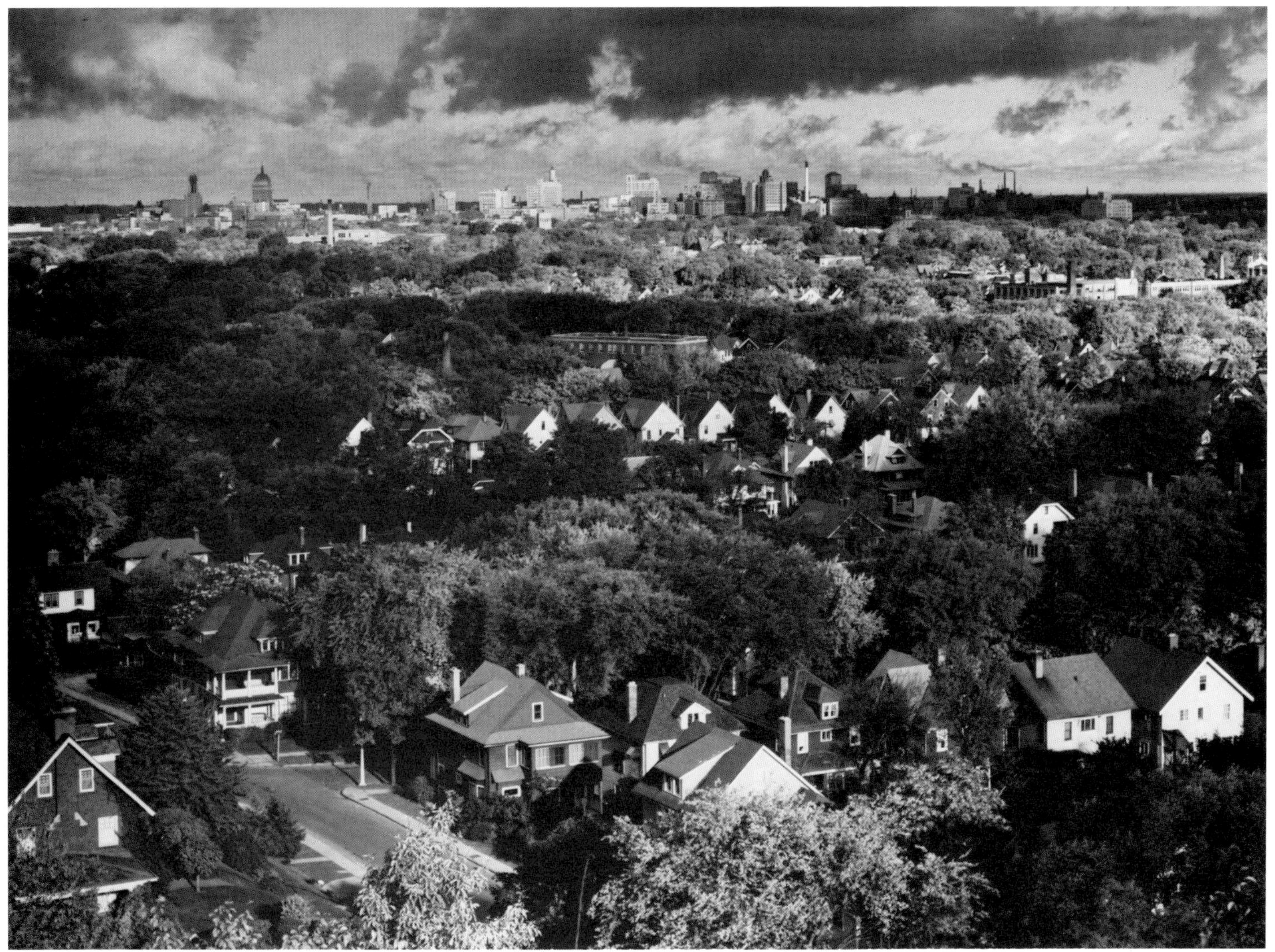

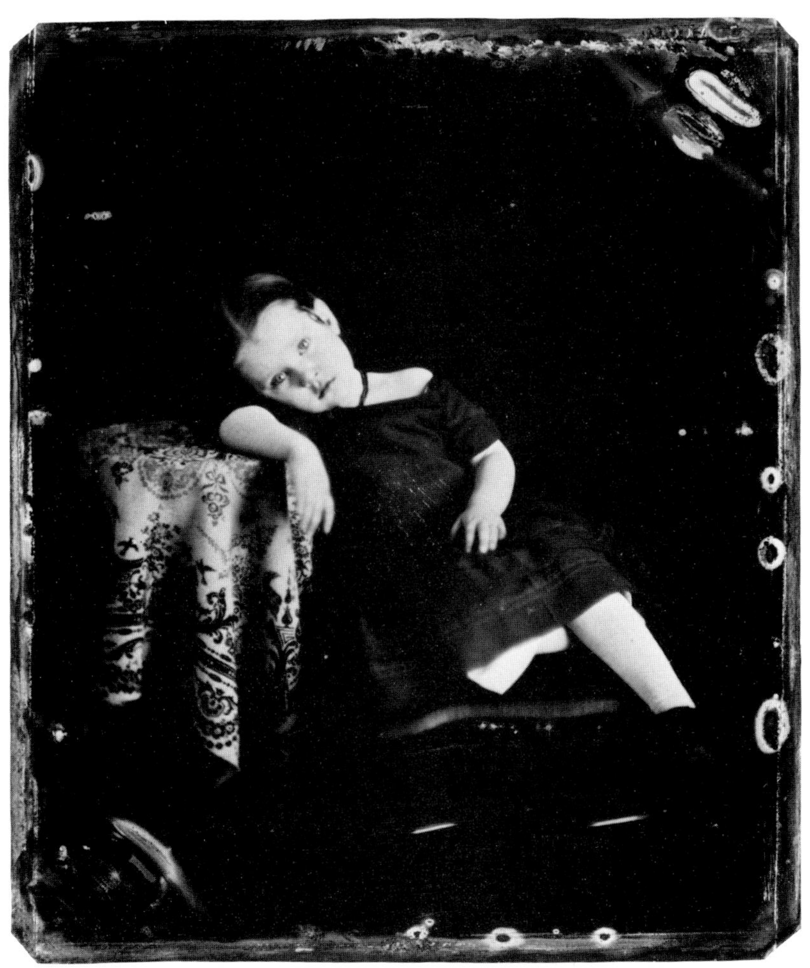 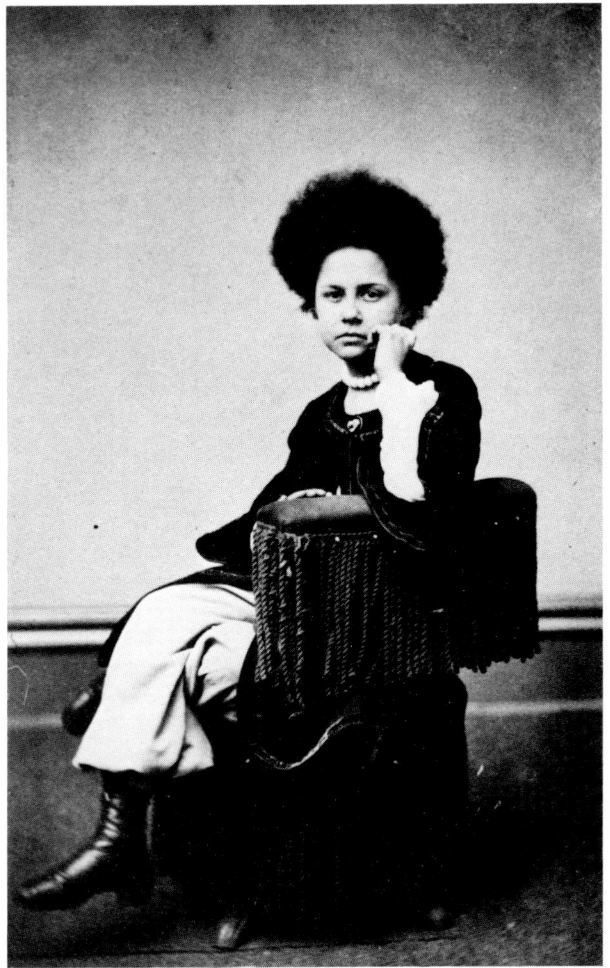

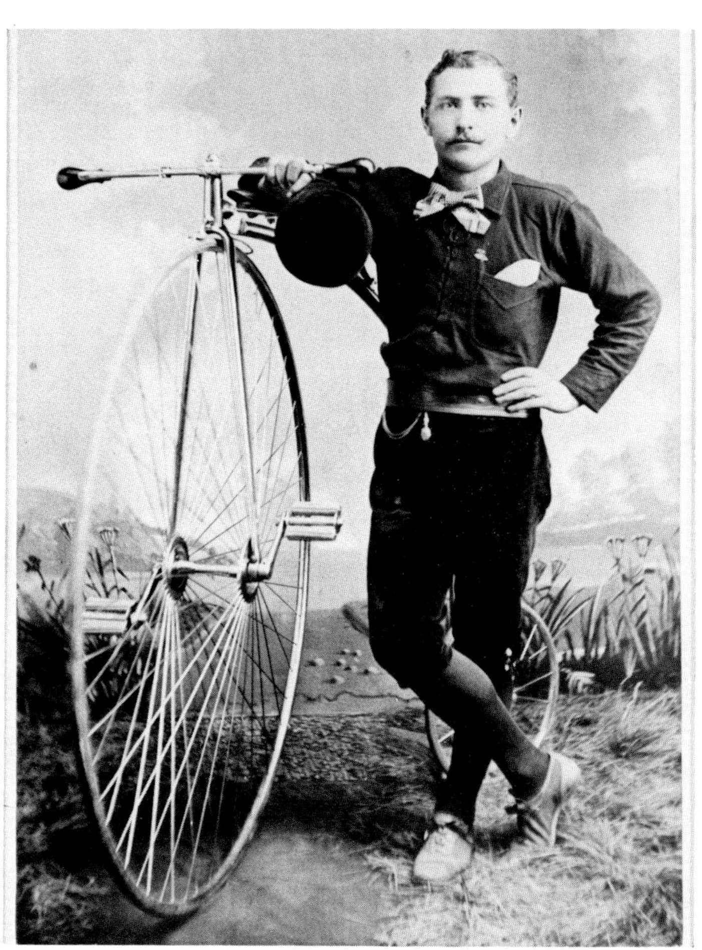

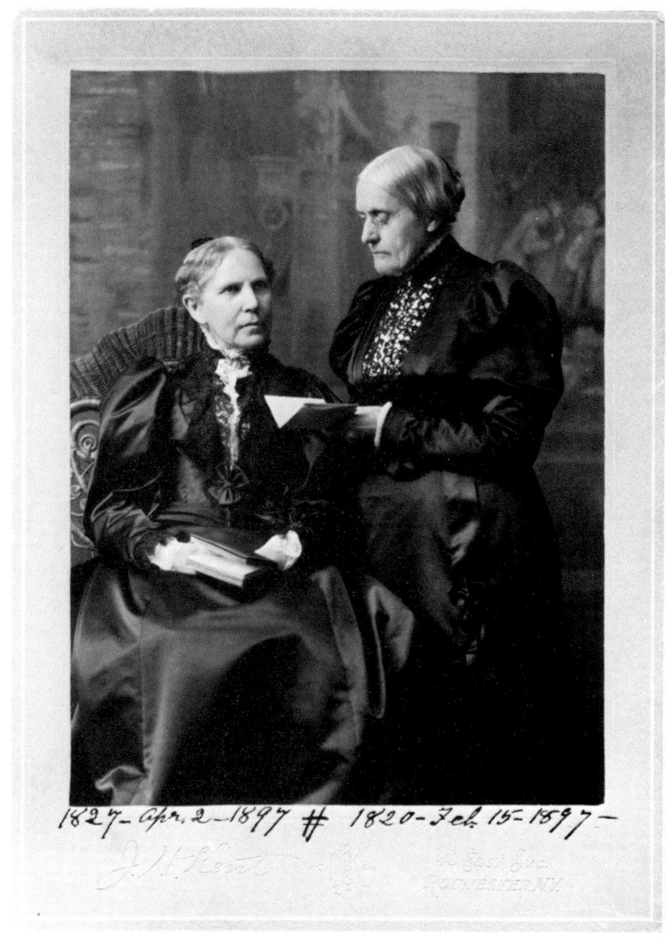

ROCHESTER
INDUSTRY
1834-1934
A CENTURY
ON PARADE

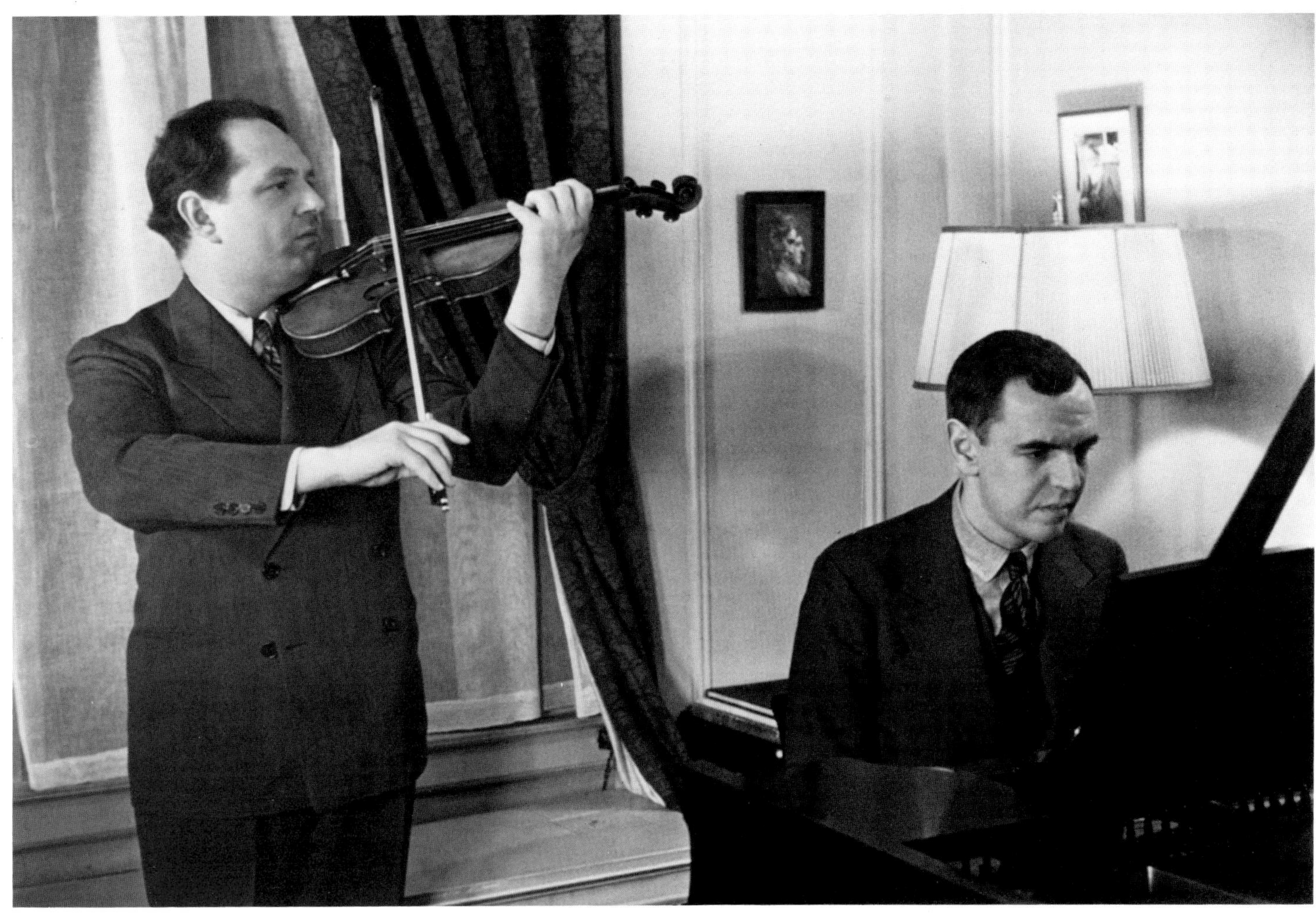

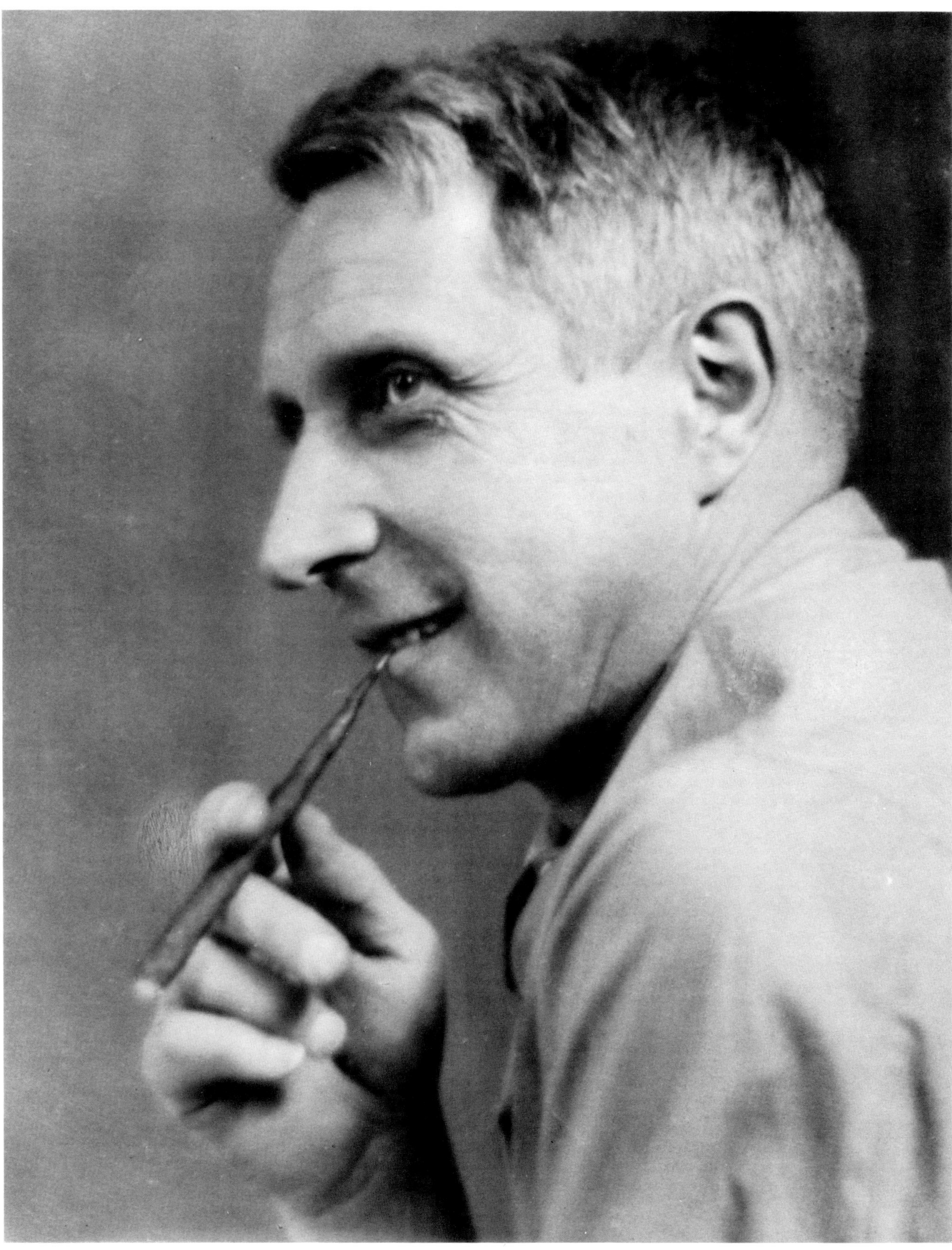

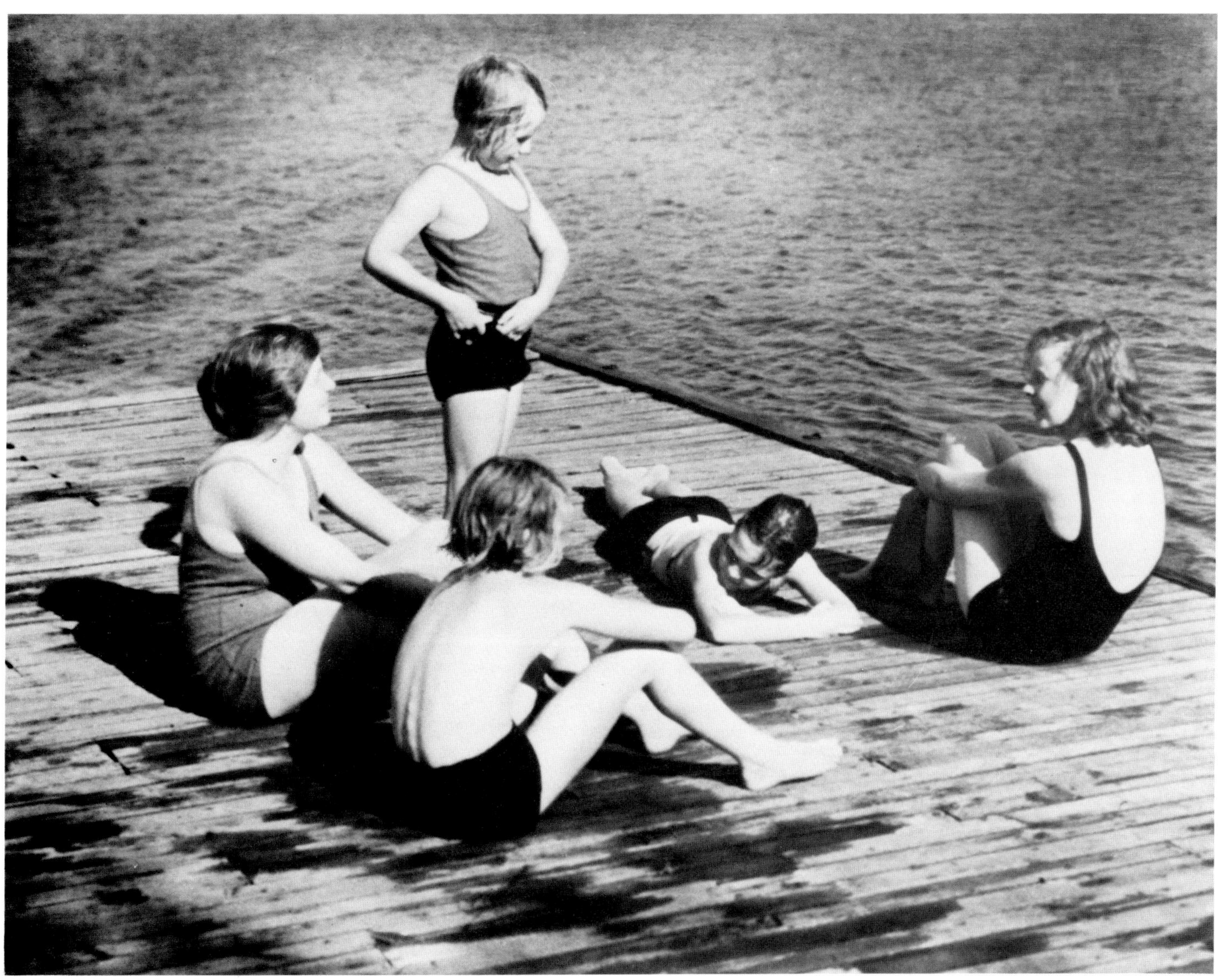

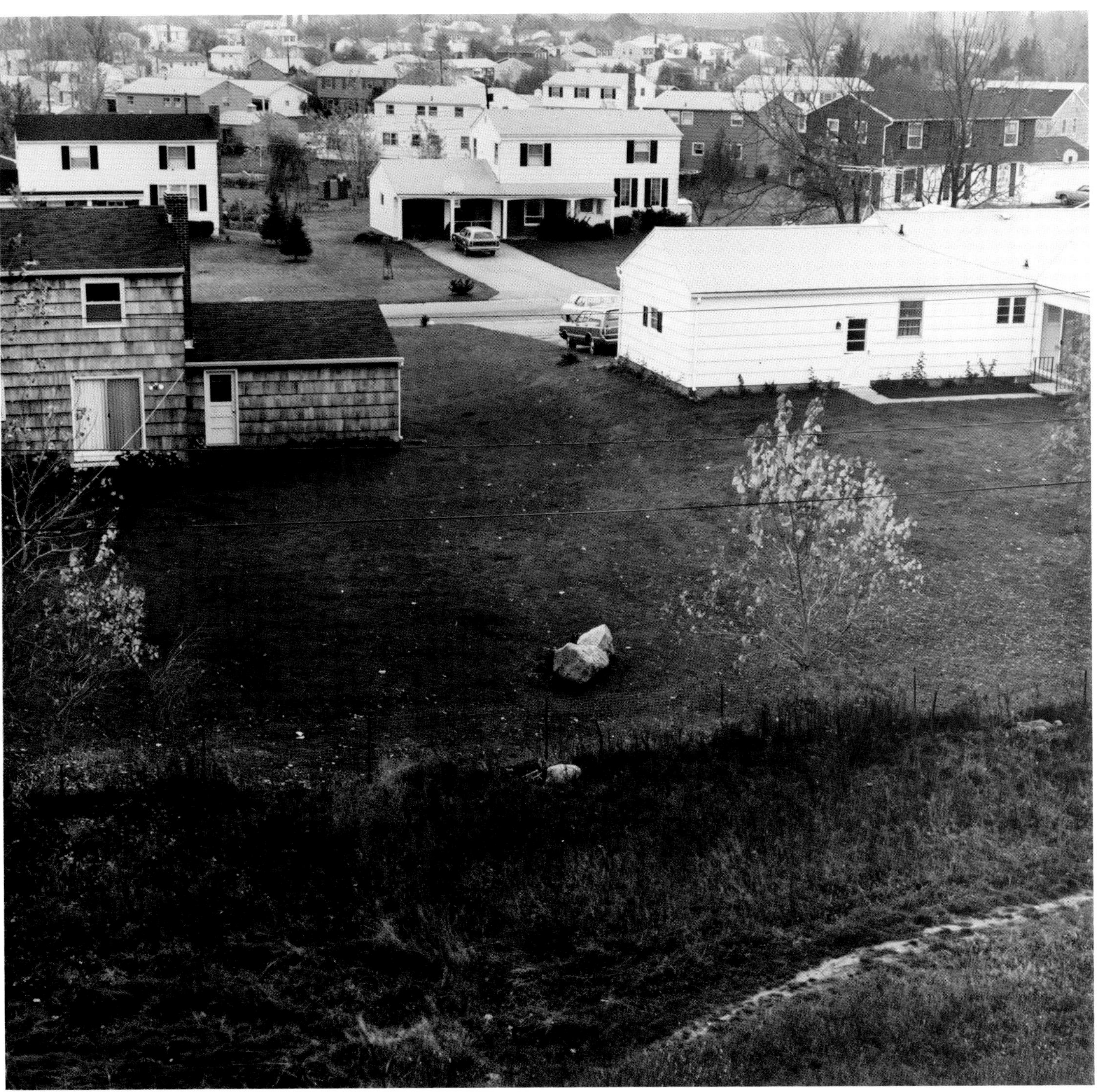

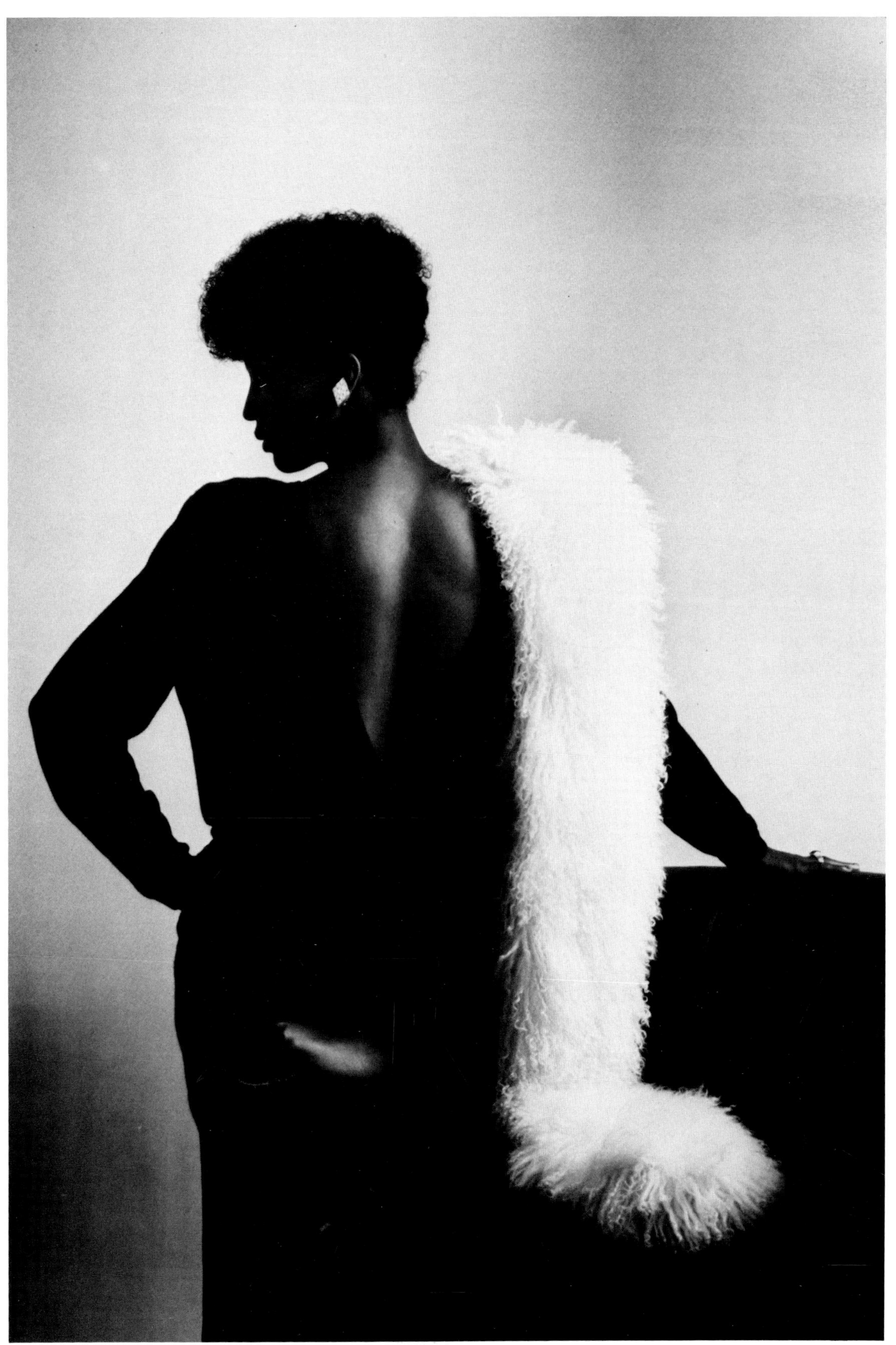

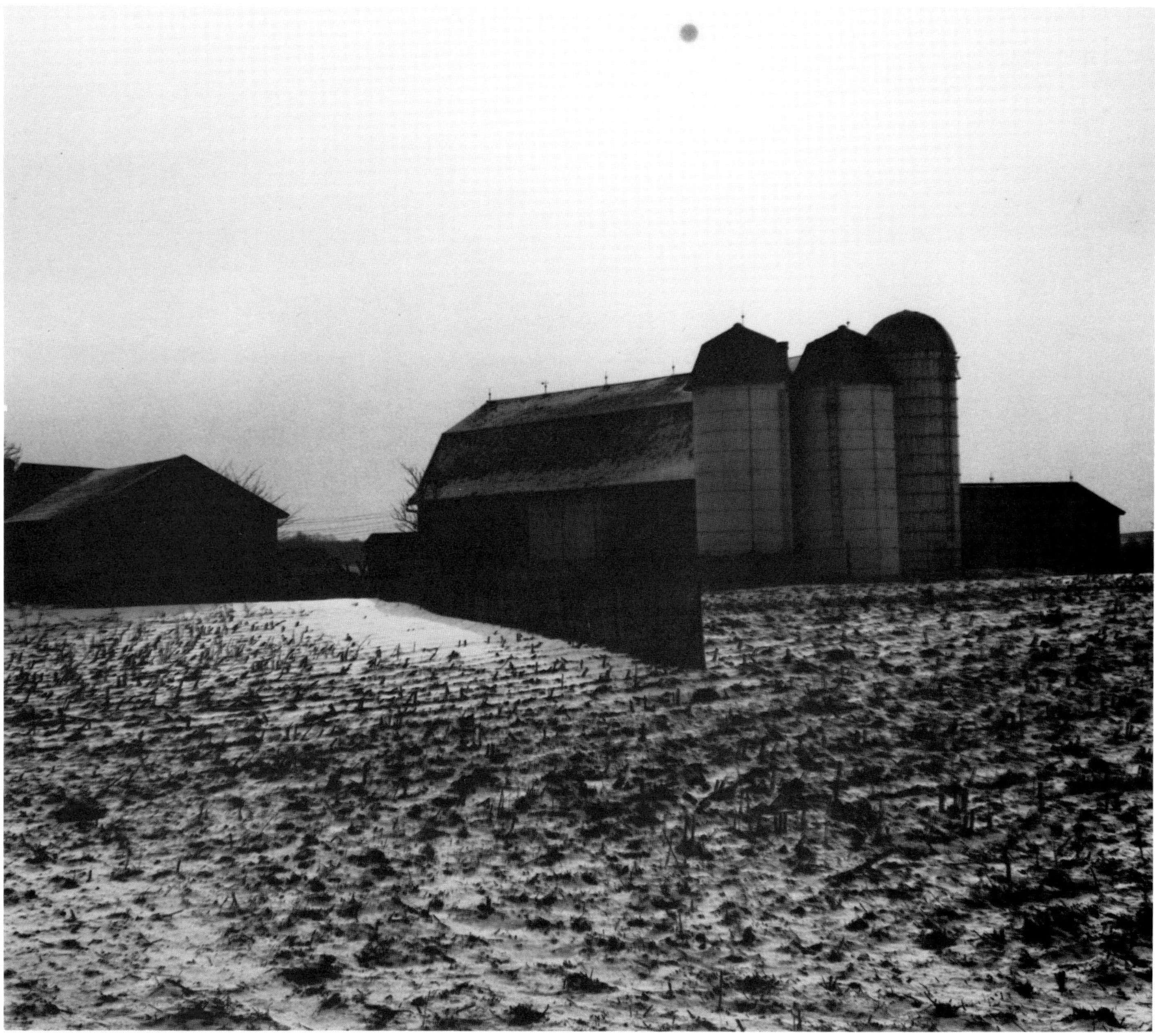

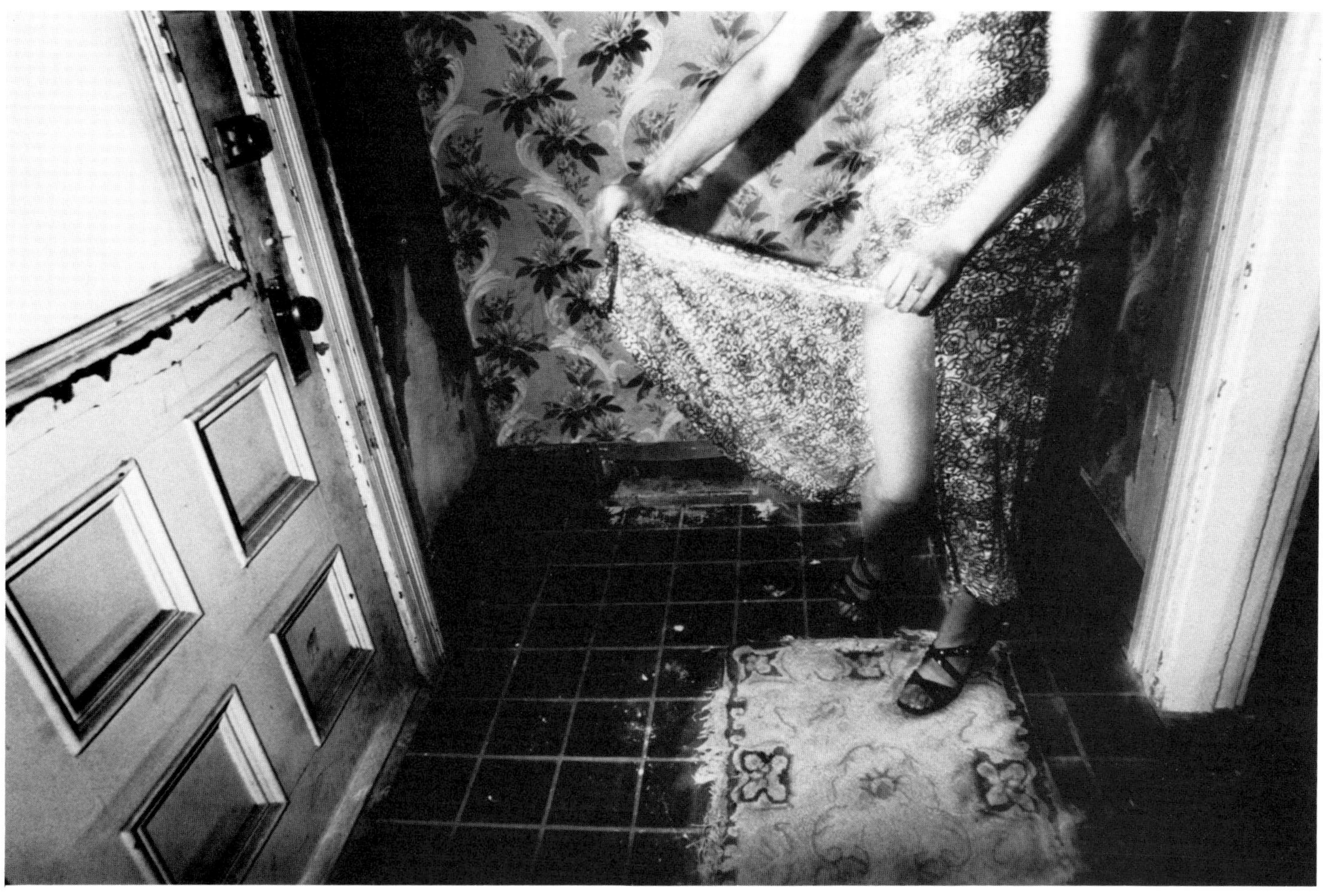

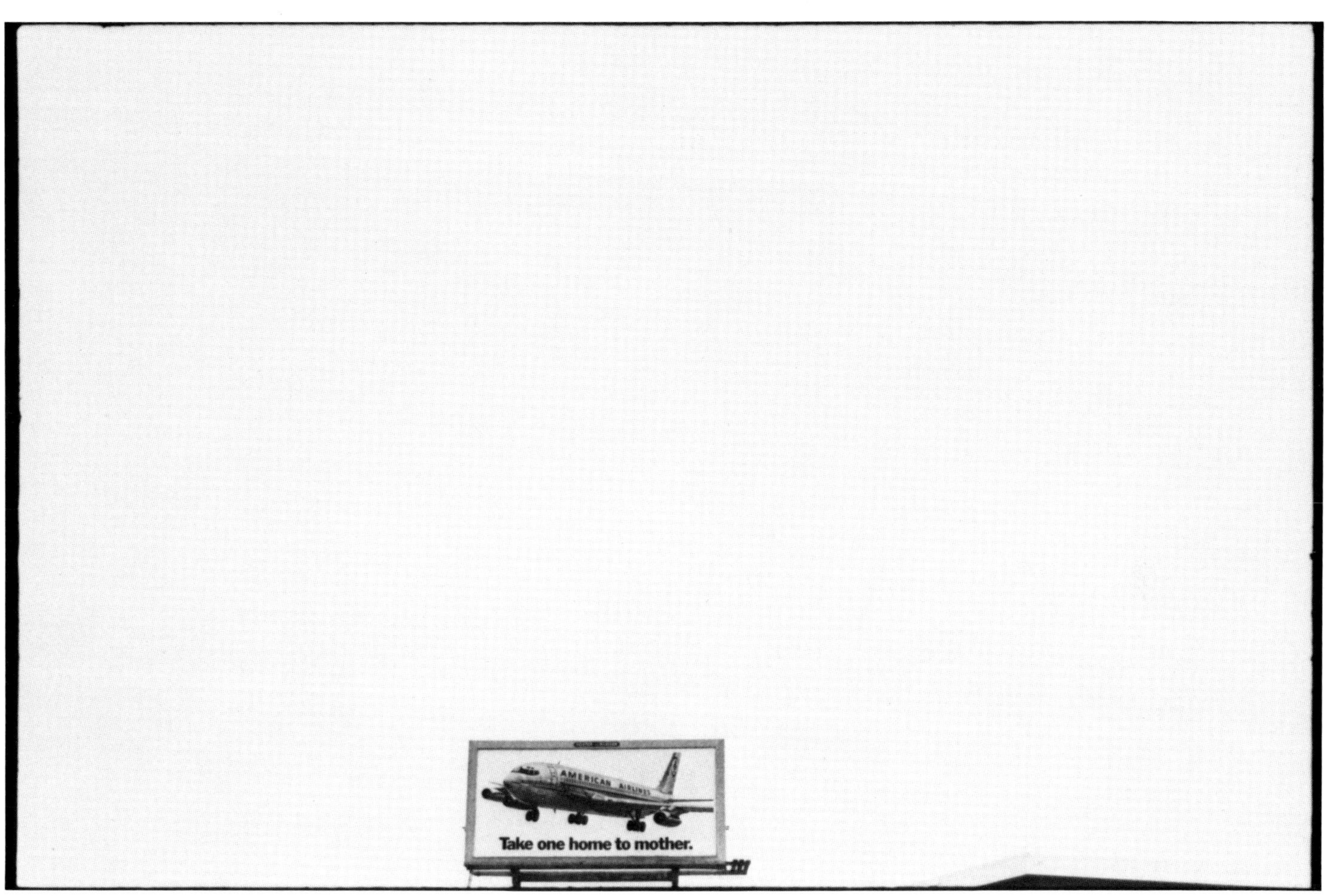
AMERICAN AIRLINES
Take one home to mother.

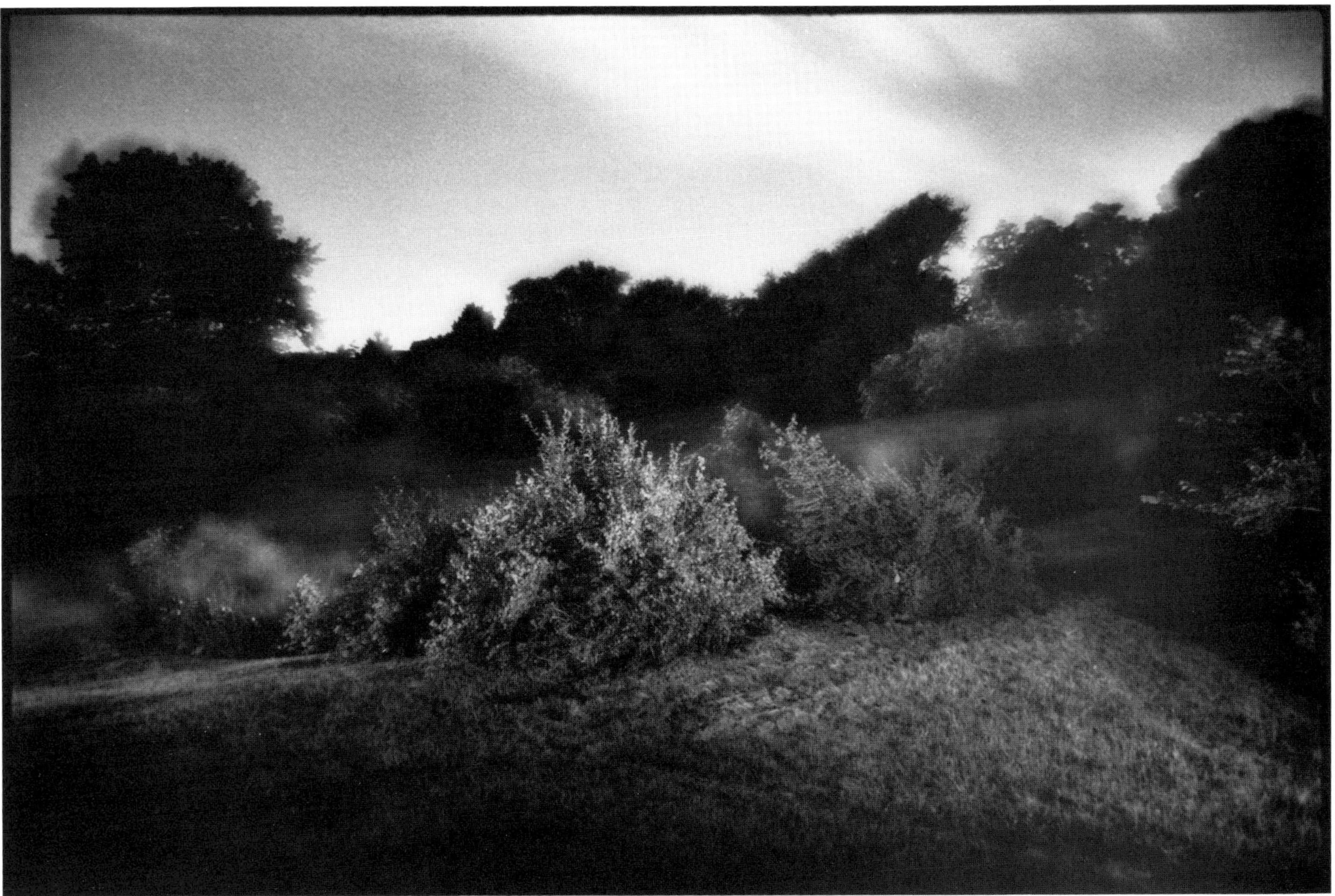

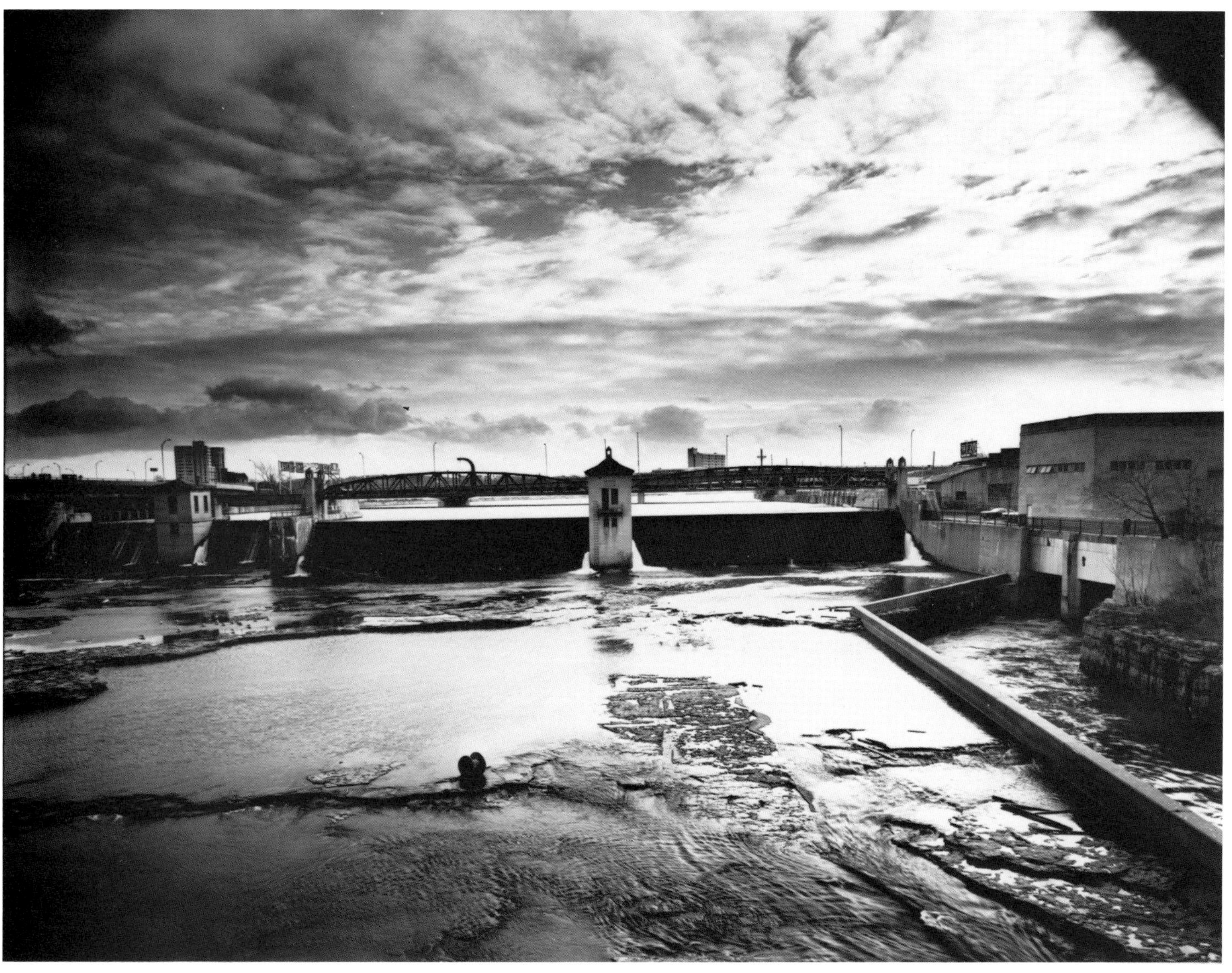

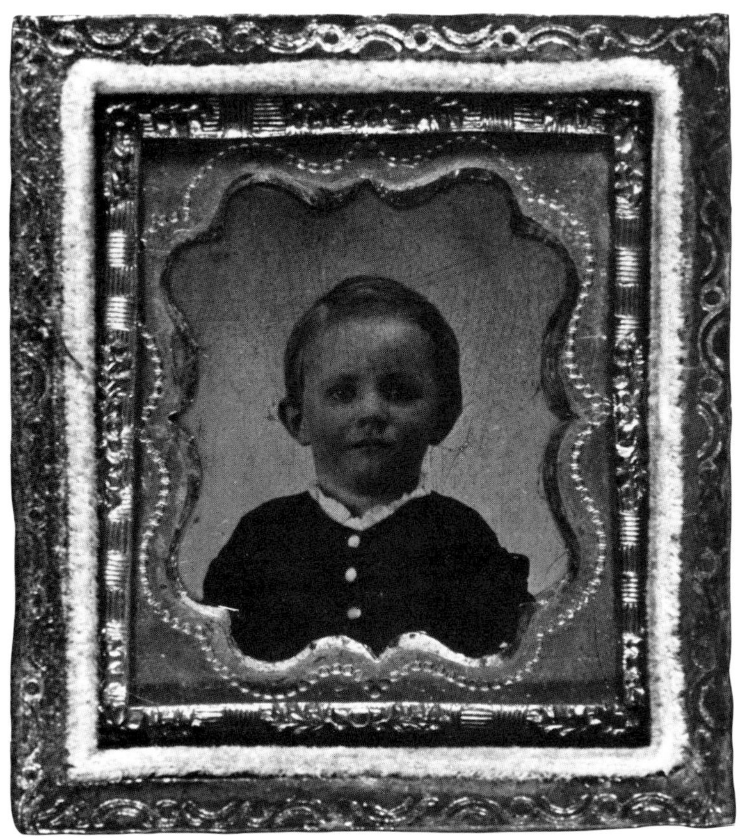

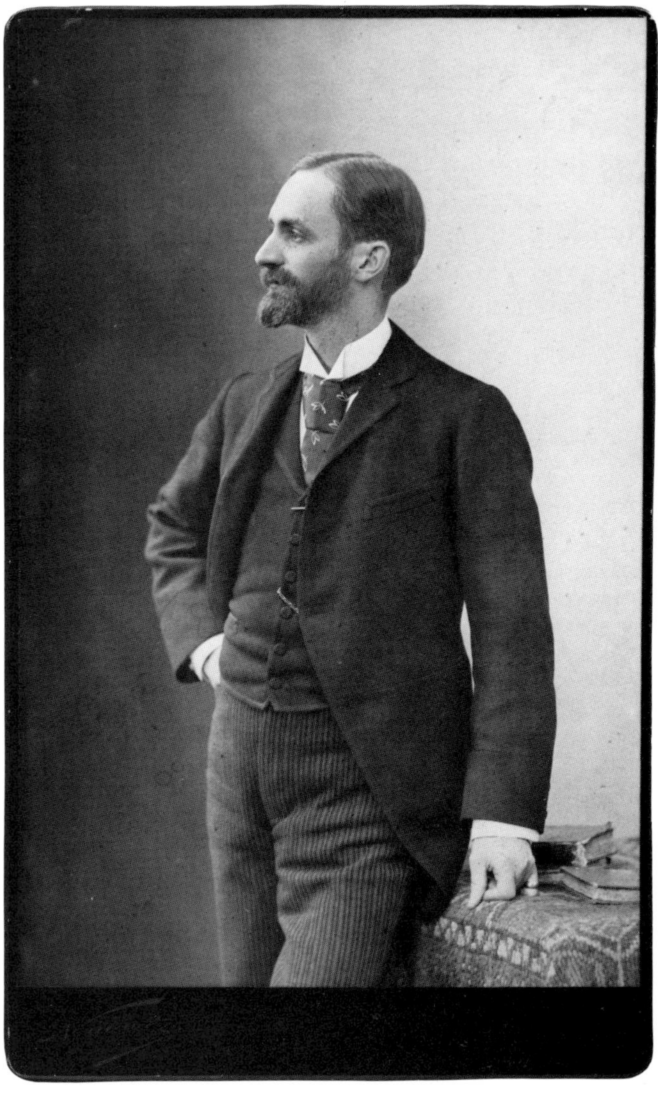

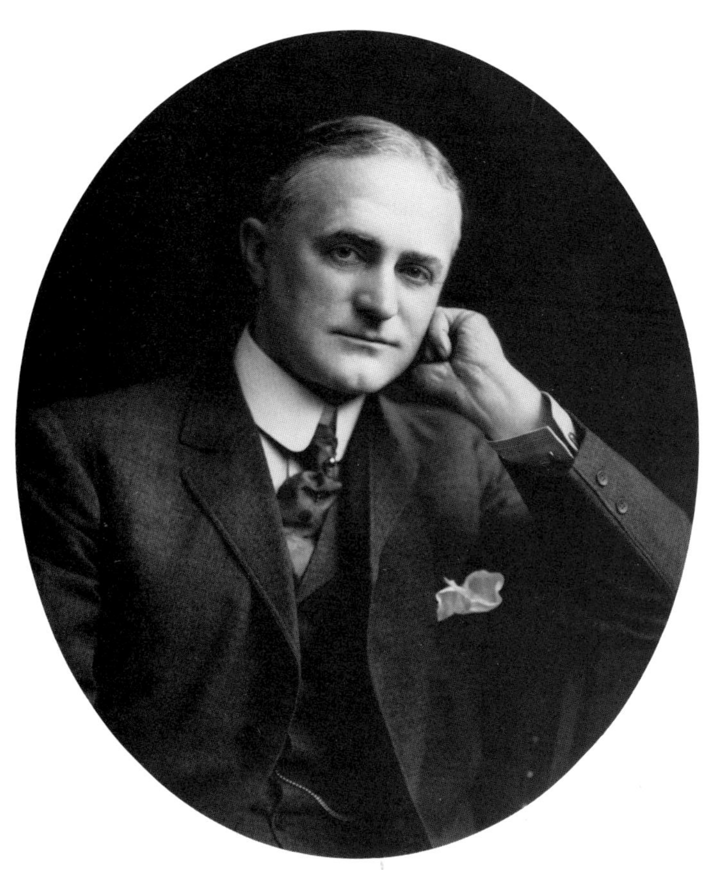

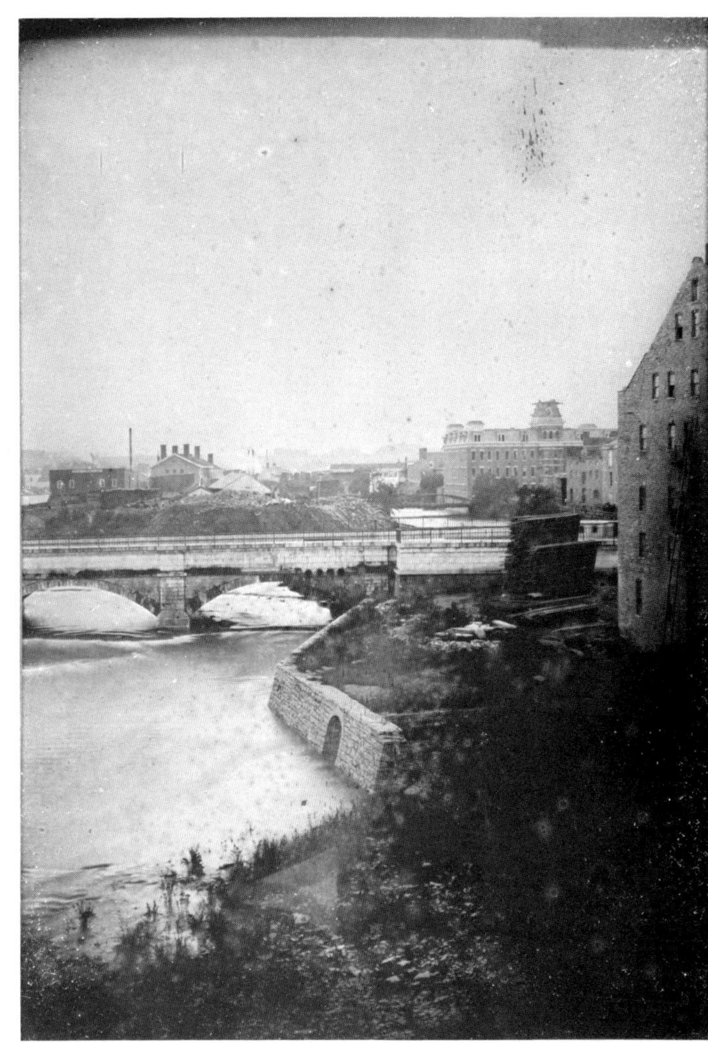

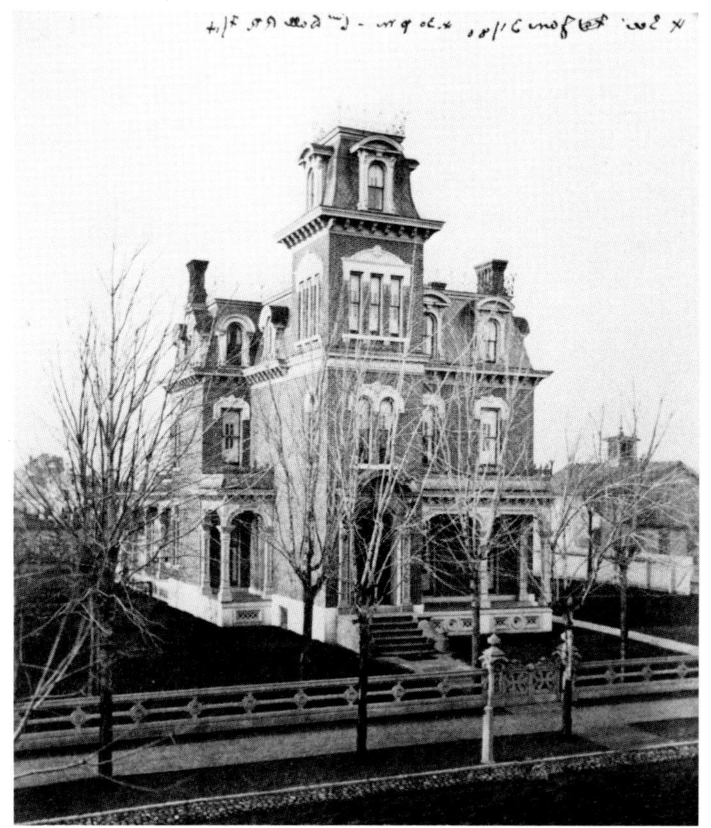

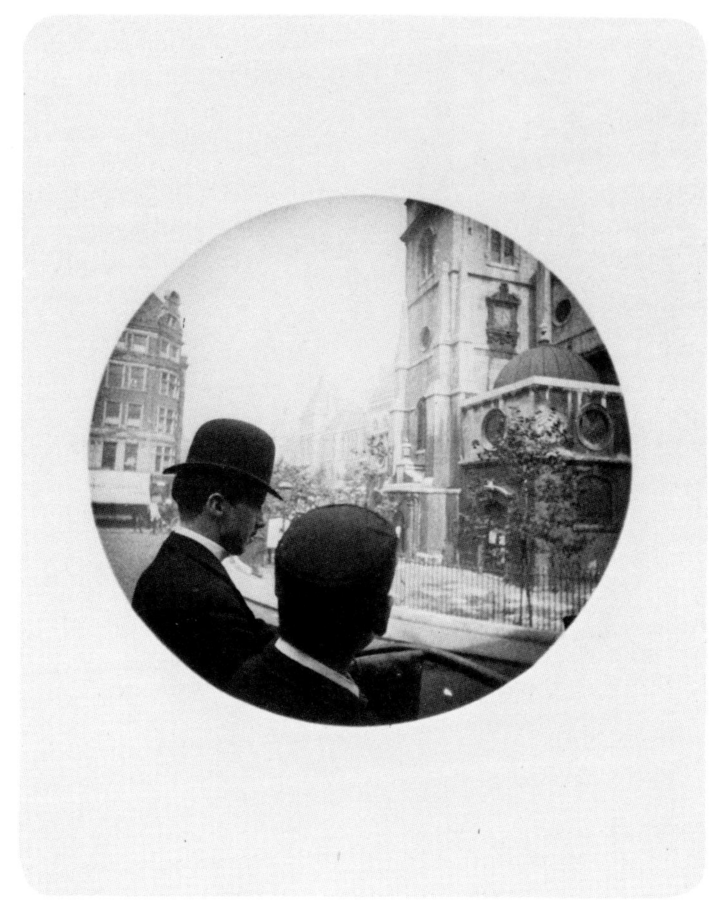

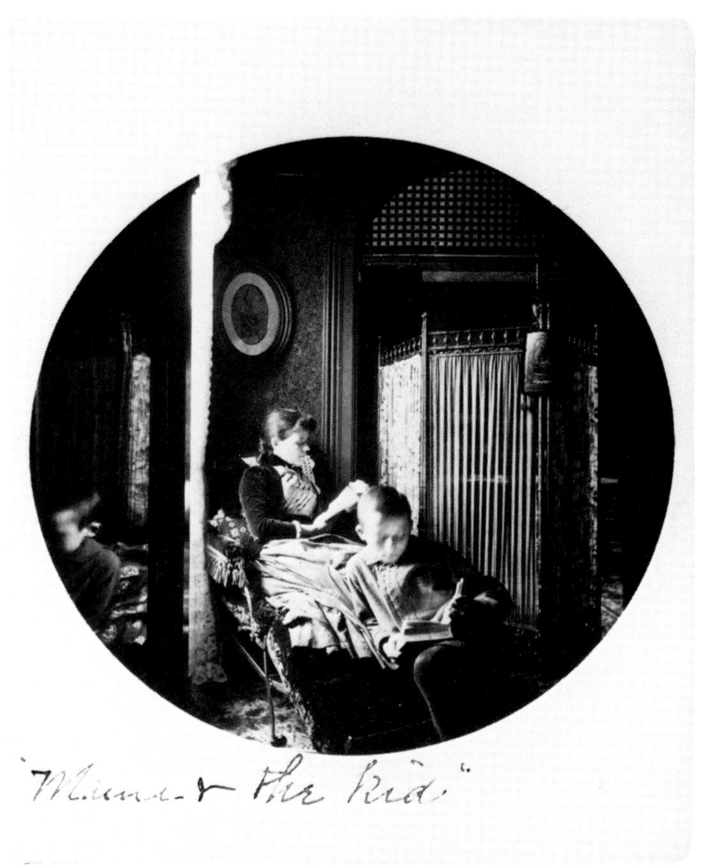
"Muma & the Kid"

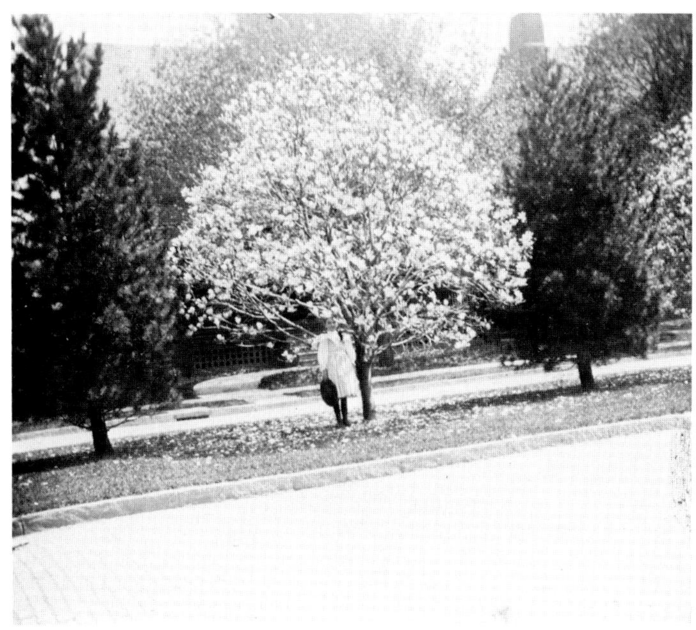

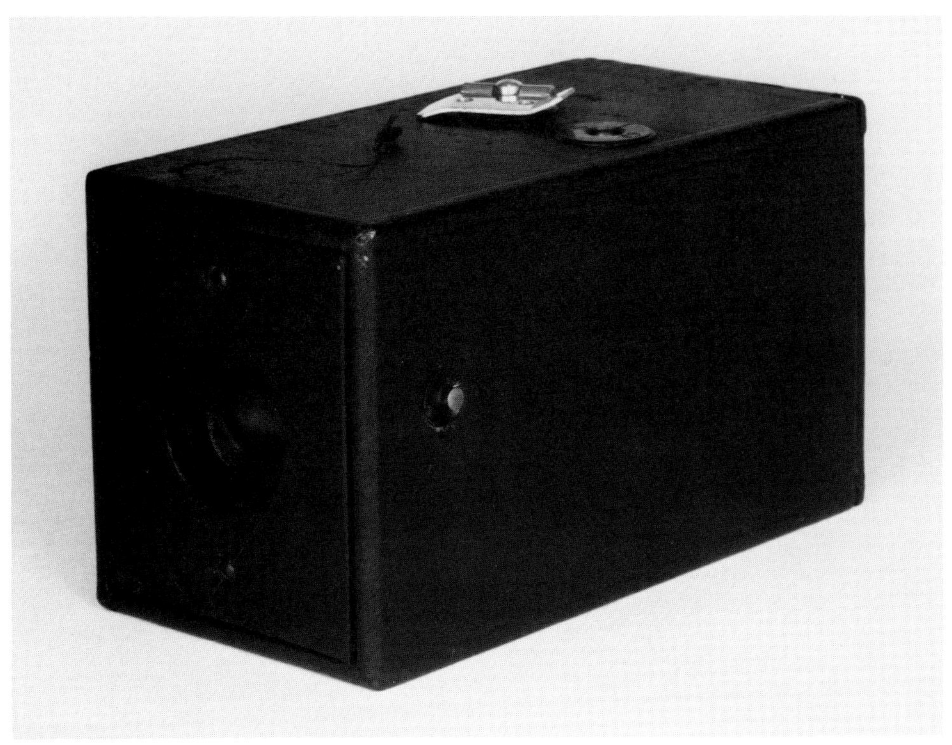

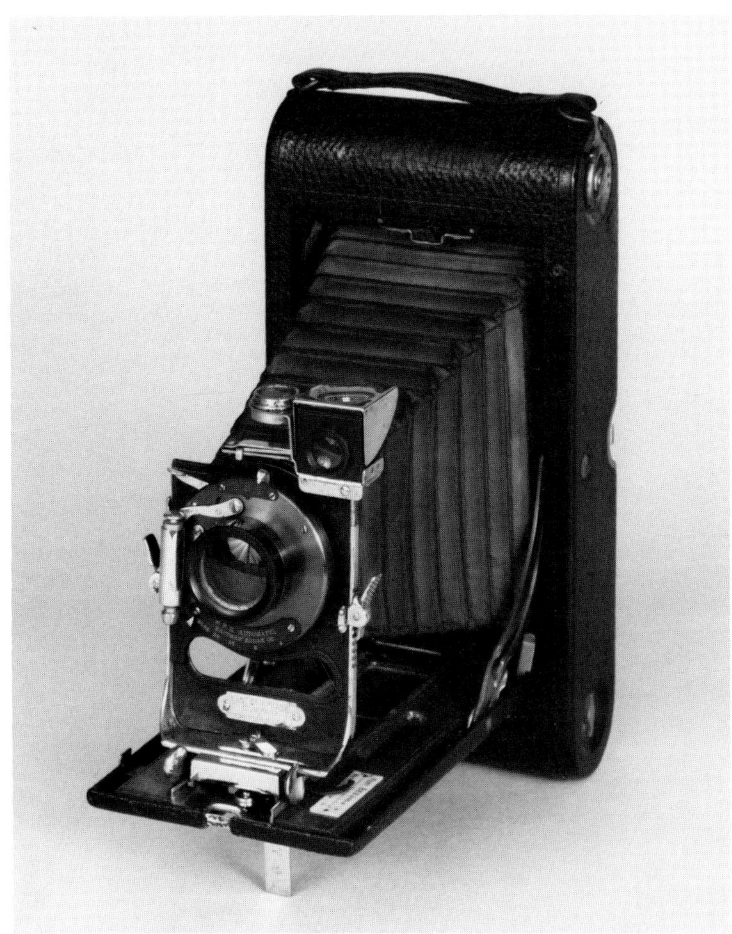

275. KODAK EKTRA (TOP)
276. CAROUSEL 550 SLIDE
PROJECTOR (CENTER)
279. KODAK DISC 4000
CAMERA (BOTTOM)

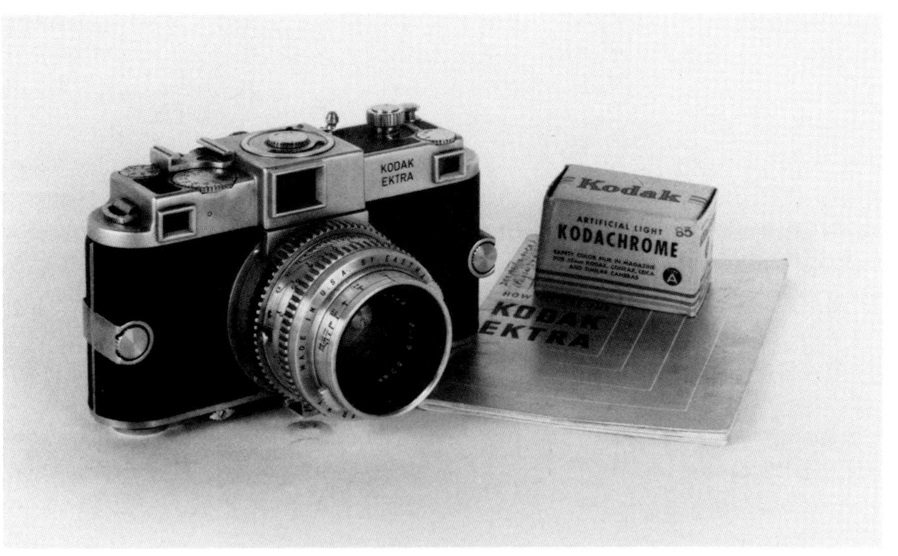

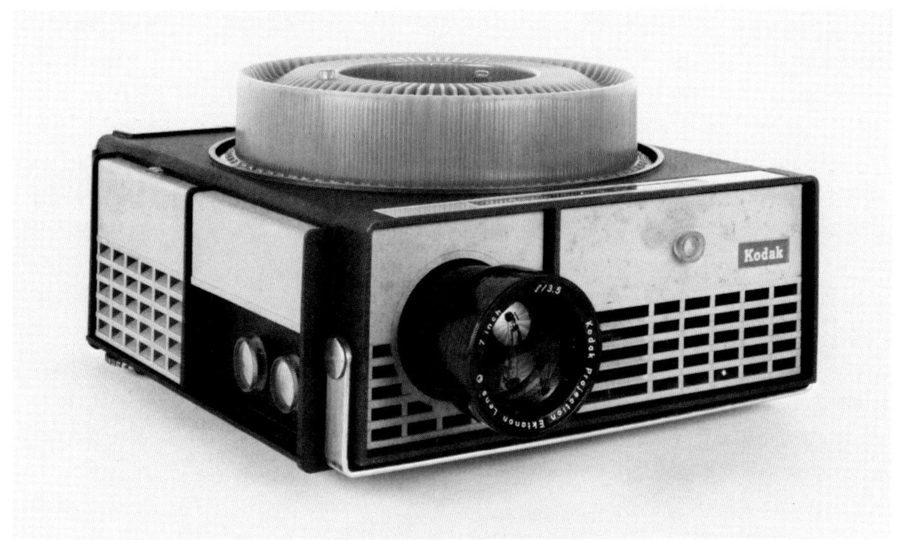

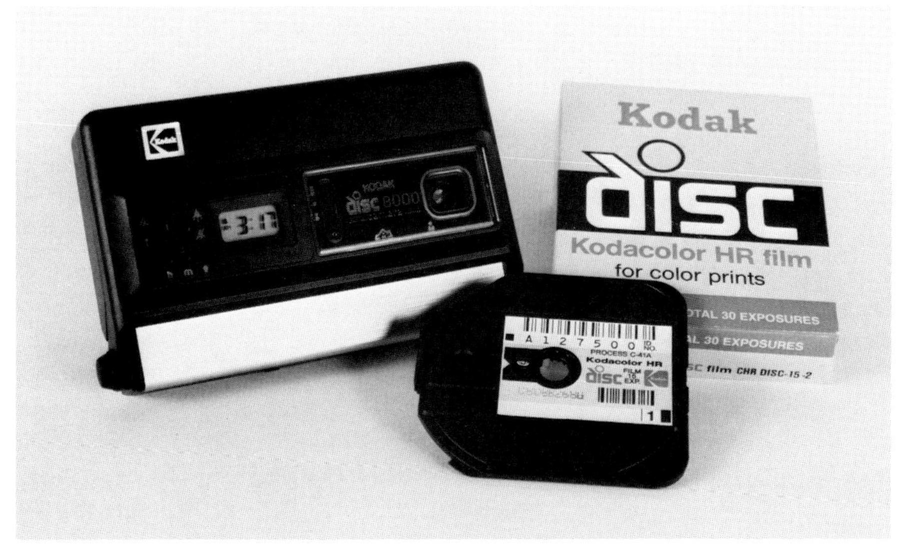

There are a variety of reasons why Rochester was an ideal location for an exciting new technology, photography, to flourish. There was a body of skilled labor, plenty of room to expand, excellent transportation facilities, and, indeed, all of the varied elements that in modern terms we call the essential infrastructure needed for development. It was the existence, however, of the right kind of entrepreneurial skills and managers able to utilize what was available that made the difference.

In 1850 John Jacob Bausch, who had been born 20 years earlier in Germany, emigrated to this country. As a teenager in Germany, he had been apprenticed to a spectacle maker who taught him the fundamentals of lens making. After several years of wandering he settled in Rochester. He worked at first as a furniture maker before setting up an optician's shop in the original Reynolds Arcade. Business was not brisk. He then met Henry Lomb, also a recent German immigrant, and they began to work together to expand the business. The partnership was formalized after the Civil War when the name of the firm became the Bausch & Lomb Optical Company.

The economic expansion of the post-Civil War era afforded the new company the opportunity to grow.

Edward Bausch, the oldest son of John Jacob Bausch, joined the firm after finishing his engineering studies at Cornell and expanded their business activities into the field of microscopes. Within a remarkably few years, Bausch & Lomb was the most eminent domestic manufacturer of microscopes and precision optical instruments.

Photographic optics were added to their product line in 1883. Although they never manufactured a complete camera, optics and shutters made by B & L were used on dozens of different camera models by many makers both in and out of Rochester. By the turn of the century they had manufactured 500,000 camera lenses and a slightly greater number of shutters, and they were making spectacles at the rate of 20 million pairs a year.

The two large red brick factory buildings on St. Paul Street, which were abandoned several years ago, were the center of the company's operations from the time of their construction during the First World War. The firm made an enormous variety of optical instruments for the war effort from searchlight mirrors to rangefinders. In order to insure an adequate domestic source of optical glass, another factory to produce this material was built on the Genesee River below

the original factory. This plant is still in operation and was the single most important source of this raw material until very recent years.

One of the more famous of post World War II products of Bausch were the optics for the widescreen cinema process known as Cinemascope. A sample of the Cinemascope Projection lens is on display in the Sesquicentennial exhibit.

The story of how George Eastman, a bookkeeper at the Rochester Savings Bank, became interested in photography and began experiments in 1879 with gelatin dry plates that were just coming into use in England has been told many times. He patented a plate-coating machine and began to make plates for sale in the loft of a building at 101 State Street. He continued his employment at the Rochester Savings Bank during these years. In 1881 he formed a partnership with Henry A. Strong, a buggy whip manufacturer. By 1882, the Eastman Dry Plate Company had six employees. The firm moved to the 343 State Street location the following year.

Eastman's first effort at producing a uniquely new product was a flexible film coated on a translucent oiled paper. Intended for use in the Eastman-Walker Roll Holder, it was replaced by a stripping film the following year.

So far all of George Eastman's products were intended to supplement and partially substitute the existing line of supplies available to the photographer. The introduction of the Kodak Camera in 1888 changed amateur photography forever. Eastman recognized that those to whom he wished to sell cameras were not interested in personal darkroom manipulation of photographic materials. The buyer of the camera received an instrument loaded with enough of Eastman's flexible film to make 100 exposures. The entire camera was returned to the factory in Rochester where the pictures were developed, printed, and mounted. The camera was reloaded and returned to the owner along with his processed pictures.

The Kodak Camera was compact, very well made, and certainly easy to use, but it was only a portion of the system created by Eastman. Far more important than this little camera was the fact that the introduction of the Kodak marked the beginning of the photo-finishing industry. Before the Kodak, there was no convenient method of having your film processed. You did it yourself or it didn't get done. The camera was sold with the motto

"You Press the Button, We Do the Rest." Although it cost $25.00, a substantial sum at the time, the camera was an instant success and was promptly followed by larger and more complex models for serious users. By the turn of the century, the Eastman Kodak Company, as it was now called, was an enormous success. Eastman had established offices in both Paris and London to market his products.

The $1.00 Brownie introduced in 1900 was even more successful than Eastman had expected. It was sold as a camera to introduce children to photography, but there were no age barriers to purchasing it. The tradenames Brownie and Kodak became the two most famous in photography.

George Eastman had a lot of competitors, so it is reasonable to ask why he succeeded while so many of them failed. Skillful management combined with massive advertising and an uncanny knack for hiring the right people were the principal pillars on which he built his organization. He was guided by the philosophical perception of the photographer as Everyman.

A detailed history of all the firms that entered and left the photographic business in Rochester would fill an enormous volume. Many companies were founded by employees who left firms to "go it alone." They combined and changed names with bewildering speed.

Ernst Gundlach, a skilled lens maker at Bausch & Lomb, left that firm in 1878 to found his own small firm to manufacture microscopes and objectives. In 1884 it was organized as the Gundlach Optical Company. For reasons that are not clear, in 1895 the same Ernst Gundlach left the firm he had founded to set up a rival company called the Gundlach Photo-Optical Company. From that date there were two Gundlach companies enjoying an independent existence in Rochester making identical products. The second firm was not much of a success. It was renamed and finally acquired by another famous name in the early years of the industry in Rochester—Wollensak.

The original Gundlach firm lived on and expanded its product line, adding shutters in 1896 and several newly designed lenses. They acquired the Manhattan Optical Company of Cresskill, New Jersey, and changed the name of the firm to the Gundlach-Manhattan Optical Company. They continued in business under different management names and declining business fortunes. The great depression was particularly hard on firms with relatively small amounts of capital and specialized product lines. The remaining assets of the firm were ultimately acquired by David Goldstein, who reorganized it, forming D.O. Industries of East Rochester, standing for Dynamic Optics, the last corporate name of the old firm.

Another spinoff from the original Bausch & Lomb management was the Wollensak Optical Company. The original goal of the new firm was the manufacture of a high-grade but reasonably priced shutter. The famous Optimo line of shutters was designed by Andrew Wollensak and sold in large numbers for more than 20 years. They added optics to their product line primarily by the purchase of the Rochester Lens Company in 1905. Like the Gundlach-Manhattan Optical Company, Wollensak had great difficulties during the depression years but survived and in 1958 was a vigorous business employing more that 1,200 persons. It then went into a steady decline and was owned first by Revere and then by 3M before finally closing down in 1972.

Yet another offshoot of B & L was the Ilex Optical Company. Two engineers who had worked for that firm invented a very important new type of shutter that for the first time allowed a shutter to be made with accurate low speeds. They founded the XL Manufacturing Company mainly to manufacture the new shutter in 1910. The firm was renamed Ilex a short time later and remained in business until very recent years. The basic patent on the Ilex shutter was so important that the rights were purchased by the German firm of Deckel, which used the design in the line of Compur shutters they produced. The German-made Compur shutter was the most famous and widely used precision design in the world. In the realm of innovation the Ilex organization can claim one other first. They invented and marketed a self-contained internal flash synchronization system, eliminating the need to use a clumsy external solenoid.

Shortly after the Second World War, three men, David L. Goldstein, Peter Terbuska, and Mortimer A. London founded the Elgeet Optical Company in a loft on Atlantic Avenue. Their principal products were an extensive line of accessory lenses for amateur motion picture equipment. The firm prospered and by the early 1950s were employing 300 people. The contraction of the amateur motion picture market caused the company fortunes to decline. David Goldstein left and acquired the assets of the former Gundlach Manufacturing Company and founded D.O. Industries. Operations were ceased in 1972.

William H. Walker, whose name was associated with George Eastman in the early years of the Eastman Dry Plate Company, had formed a company in the same year as Eastman to manufacture a small camera and glass plates. Walker remained with the firm only briefly, sold his share of the company he had founded and went to work for Eastman. The Eastman-Walker Roll Holder was a product of this new relationship. Walker's firm was purchased by W. F. Carlton, who founded the Rochester Optical Company using the assets he had acquired as a base.

The Rochester Optical Company went through an almost Byzantine series of changes in ownership and name before it was finally purchased by the Eastman Kodak Company, at which time it became the Rochester Optical Department.

At the same time that George Eastman was preparing to market his Kodak Camera in 1888, William F. Folmer and William E. Schwing of New York City established a firm to manufacture and market bicycles. In the early years they marketed but did not actually manufacture cameras.

Folmer, an engineer, built the first Graflex camera in 1898. The first model was fitted with a variable aperture-type of focal plane shutter and was very troublesome. The classic Graflex focal plane shutter, a very simple and rugged design, was introduced in 1904 and remained in production for more than 60 years. This is a record for a product of this type.

In 1905, George Eastman purchased outright the assets of the Folmer & Schwing Manufacturing Company and moved the firm to Rochester. For the next 20 years it operated as a division of Eastman Kodak. In 1926 Eastman Kodak was ordered to divest itself of its holdings in the Graflex organization. The courts determined that it monopolized camera manufacture in this country, thus violating the Sherman Anti-Trust Act. The Folmer Graflex Corporation was formed in that year. The name was changed to just Graflex, Inc. in 1945. Some of the most famous cameras in the world were manufactured by Graflex. The Speed Graphic was the badge of press photographers and was frequently more useful than a press pass as an admittance ticket to important events. The large-format Graflex Single Lens Reflex cameras were on the market for nearly six decades. During the war, Graflex manufactured a

variety of special cameras for the military. Business began a slow but steady decline as improved films shifted photographers to smaller-format cameras. The firm was acquired by General Precision Instruments in 1956 and ten years later by Singer. Graflex was in business making audio-visual equipment until a few years ago. Nothing of consequence remains of the original firm.

A few words should be said about Frank A. Brownell. The June 1983 issue of Image magazine, published by the International Museum of Photography at George Eastman House, featured an article about Mr. Brownell written by his grandson, Frank Brownell Mehlenbacher. Frank Brownell manufactured all of the cameras marketed by the Eastman Kodak Company for about 20 years. Prior to his years working under contract with Eastman, Frank Brownell operated the firm of F. A. Brownell, Manufacturer, and made a variety of professional studio cameras. Mr. Mehlenbacher has been kind enough to lend for this special exhibit the only known example of a Brownell Camera, the stereo model on display with a variety of early Eastman products.

Apart from Eastman Kodak and Bausch & Lomb there are nearly a dozen firms in the Rochester area engaged in the manufacture of optical products for the photographic industry. The two most important in this area are Tropel, Inc. and D.O. Industries in East Rochester. Employing about 250 persons, Tropel is a very active optical design firm as well as a manufacturer of a variety of specialized optical systems. D.O. Industries, as mentioned earlier, was formed out of the residual assets of the old Gundlach-Manhattan Optical Company and makes a variety of lens systems, including projection optics and optical laser systems.

Philip L. Condax
Director, Technology
Collections

FILM, PLATES AND PAPER

G. Eastman	1878-1881
Eastman Dry Plate Company	1881-1884
Eastman Dry Plate and Film Company	1884-1889
The Eastman Company	1889-1892
Eastman Kodak Company	1892-present
George H. Monroe	1882-1889
C. and V. E. Forbes	1883-1893
Victor E. Forbes	1893-1907
Walker, Reid and Inglis	1882-1883
Inglis and van Voorhees	1883-1889
Photo Materials Company	1892-1900
Defender Dry Plate Company	1899-1945
DuPont Film Company	1945-present
Haloid Company	1906-1959
Haloid Xerox	1959-1961
Xerox Corporation	1961-present
Wilmot Corporation	1925-1926

PHOTOGRAPHIC LENSES

Bausch and Lomb Optical Company	1883-1939?
Gundlach Optical Company	1884-1902
Gundlach-Manhattan Optical Company	1902-1927
Seebold Invisible Camera Company	1927-1934
Gundlach Manufacturing Company	1933-1935; 1938-1968
Gundlach Photo-Optical Company	1895-1896
E. Gundlach, Lens Manufacturer	1896-1897
E. Gundlach, Son and Company	1897-1898
Rochester Lens Company	1898-1905
Vogt Optical Company	1899-1901
Wollensak Optical Company	1902-1972
Crown Optical Company	1906-1919
Ilex Optical Company	1911-1979
Eastman Kodak Company	1913-present
Projection Optics Company	1918-present

CAMERA MANUFACTURERS

William H. Walker	1880-1883
Frank A. Brownell	1883-1885
for Eastman	1885-1902
Rochester Optical Company	1883-1899
Rochester Camera Manufacturing Company	1891-1895
Rochester Camera Company	1895-1897
Rochester Camera & Supply Company	1897-1899
Gustave D. Milburn	1891-1892; 1894-1896
Photo Materials Company	1892-1894
Sunart Photo Company	1893-1900
Mutschler, Robertson & Company	1894-1896
Ray Camera Company	1896-1899
Gundlach Optical Company	1896-1902
Gundlach-Manhattan Optical Company	1902-1927
Seebold Invisible Camera Company	1927-1934
Gundlach Manufacturing Company	1933-1935; 1938-1968
Reichenbach, Morey and Will	1896-1900
Monroe Camera Company	1896-1899
Gassner and Marx Camera Company	1898-1899
Rochester Optical and Camera Company	1899-1903
Blair Camera Company	1899-1907
Blair Div. of Eastman Kodak	1907-1913
Seneca Camera Company	1899-1926
Century Camera Company	1900-1907
Century Div. of Eastman Kodak	1907-1917
Graf-Comppen Company	1902-1903
Eastman Kodak Company	1902-present
Rochester Optical Company (II)	1903-1907
Rochester Optical Div. of Eastman Kodak	1907-1917
Rochester Optical Dept. of Eastman Kodak	1917-1922
Rochester Panoramic Camera Company	1904-1905
Folmer and Schwing Manufacturing Company	1905-1907
Folmer and Schwing Div. of Eastman Kodak	1907-1917
Folmer-Century Div. of Eastman Kodak	1917-1926
Folmer Graflex Corporation	1926-1945
Graflex, Inc.	1945-1956
Mechanics Manufacturing Company	1909-1911
Movette Camera Corporation	1916-1926

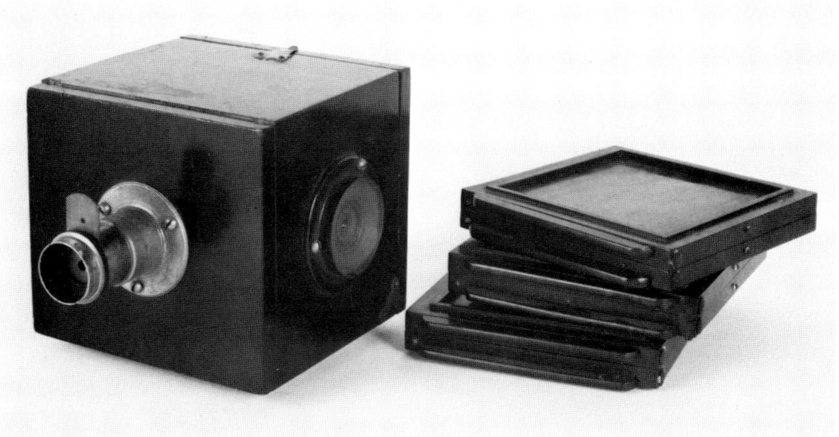

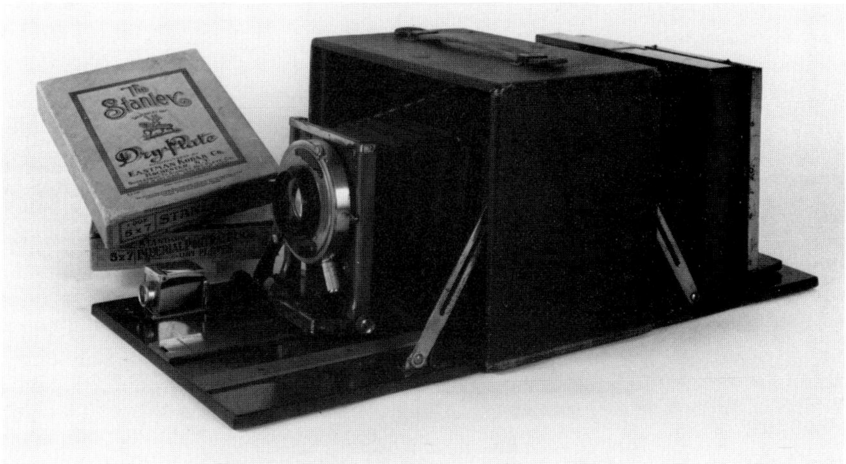

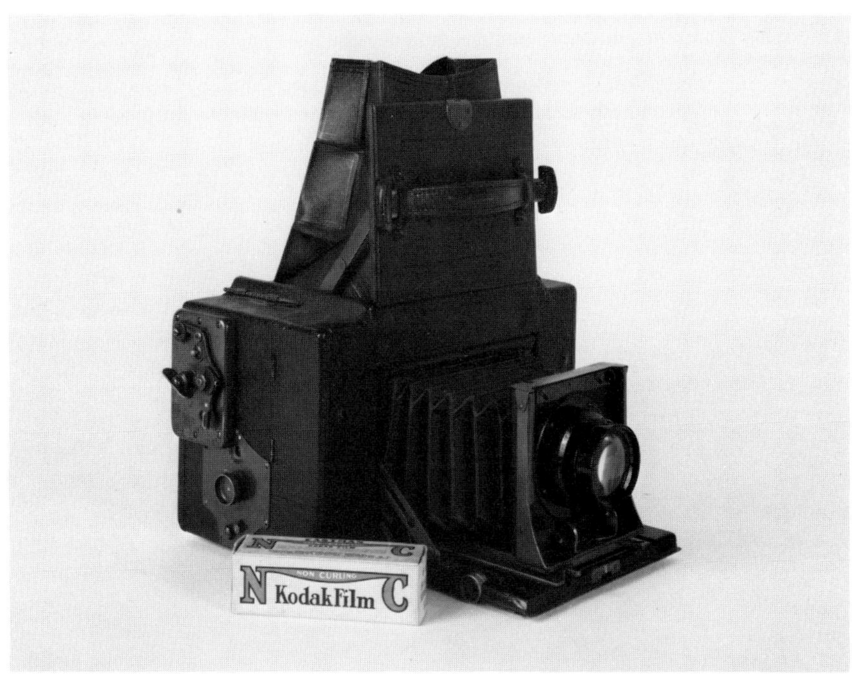
N Kodak Film C

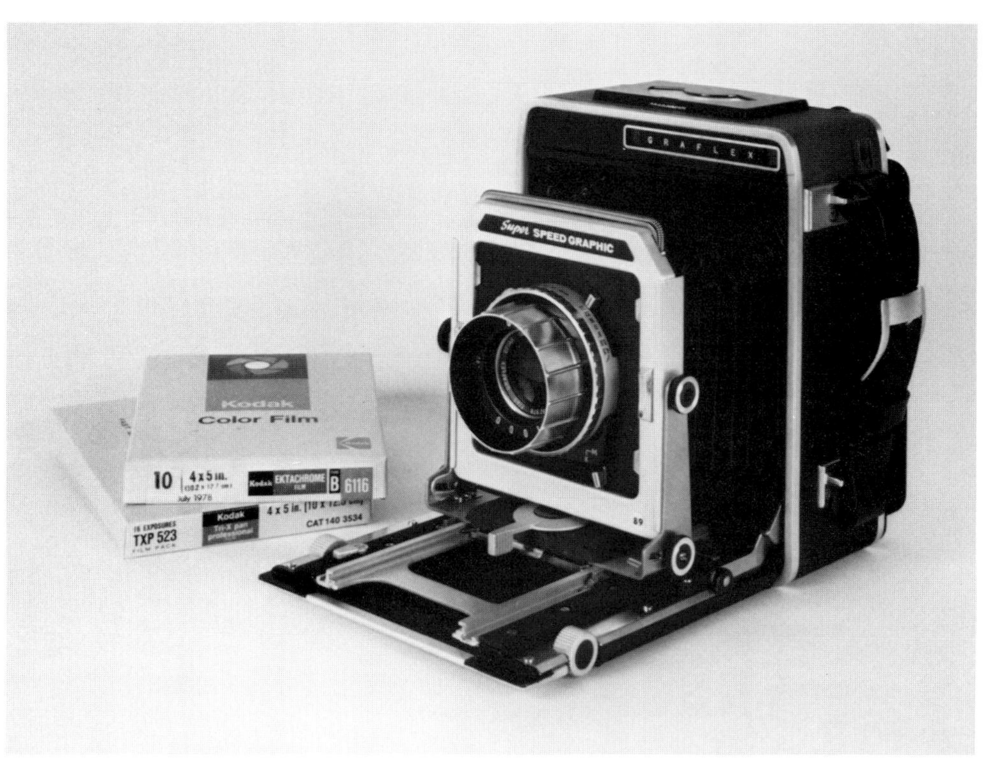

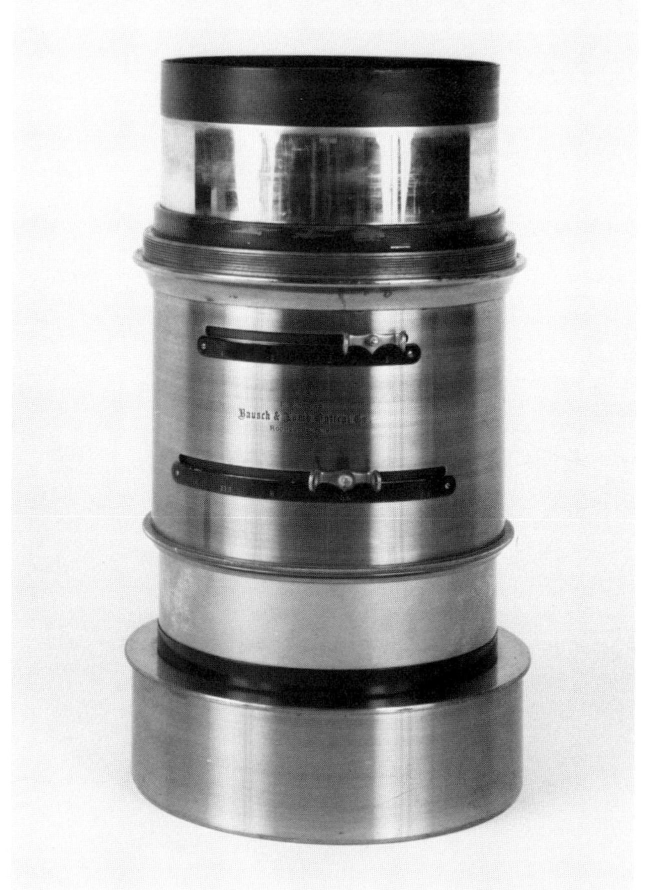

PREHISTORY

1.
CAPTAIN BASIL HALL
British (1788–1844)
The Village of Rochester
1827
from: Captain Basil Hall, Forty
    Etchings from Sketches made
    with the Camera Lucida in
    North America, in 1827 and
    1828. Edinburgh and London,
    1829.
Etching
12.0 x 20.5 cm.
76:0296:10
Gift of Emerson Tuttle

BEGINNINGS (1839–1865)

2.
EDWARD TOMPKINS WHITNEY
(1820–?) (active 1845–1858 +)
[Unidentified female]
ca. 1851-53
Daguerreotype, applied color
Sixth plate
68:0097:18
Gift of Miss M. Stone Bush

3.
EDWARD TOMPKINS WHITNEY
(1820–?) (active 1845–1858 +)
[Unidentified female child]
ca. 1851-53
Daguerreotype, applied color
Sixth plate
68:0097:17
Gift of Miss M. Stone Bush

4.
EDWARD TOMPKINS WHITNEY
(1820–?) (active 1845–1858 +)
[Unidentified male]
ca. 1851-53
Daguerreotype, applied color
Sixth plate
79:3269:3
Gift of Morris Staples

5.
EDWARD TOMPKINS WHITNEY
(1820–?) (active 1845–1858 +)
[Unidentified male child]
ca. 1851-53
Daguerreotype, applied color
Sixth plate
68:0097:25
Gift of Miss M. Stone Bush

6.
EDWARD TOMPKINS WHITNEY
(1820–?) (active 1845–1858 +)
[Unidentified male and female]
ca. 1851-53
Daguerreotype, applied color
Sixth plates, 2 daguerreotypes in
    case
72:0225:1, 2
Museum collection, by exchange

7.
EDWARD TOMPKINS WHITNEY
(1820–?) (active 1845–1858 +)
"Standing: Roswell Hart, Louise,
    Henry. Seated: Jane Hart, Anna
    Mumford, Henry Eli Rochester
    (youngest son of Nathaniel
    Rochester), Fanny Cooper"
1852
Daguerreotype
Whole plate
70:0095:1
Museum collection

8.
EDWARD TOMPKINS WHITNEY
(1820–?) (active 1845–1858 +)
[Corner of State and Main Streets,
    Rochester, New York]
ca. 1852
Daguerreotype
Whole plate
79:3275:1
Museum purchase

9.
RICHARD B. APPLEBY
(active 1851–1859 +)
Class of 1854
1854
Daguerreotype
Composite, 20 sixth plates and 1
    whole plate in frame
75:0026:1
Gift of Miriam Rogachefsky

10.
EDWARD TOMPKINS WHITNEY
(1820–?) (active 1845–1858 +)
[Man in vagabond clothes]
ca. 1854
Ambrotype, applied color
Half plate
73:0062:4
Museum collection

11.
RICHARD B. APPLEBY
(active 1851–1859 +)
Class of 1856
1856
Ambrotype
Composite, 18 quarter plates in
    frame
75:0026:2
Gift of Miriam Rogachefsky

12.
D. HOVEY and HENRY
    HARTMAN
(active 1857–1863)
[Unidentified male]
ca. 1862
Albumen print
Carte-de-visite, 9.5 x 5.6 cm.
69:0184:37
Gift of Ruth L. Works

13.
D. HOVEY and HENRY
    HARTMAN
(active 1857–1863)
[Unidentified male]
ca. 1863
Albumen print
Carte-de-visite, 4.8 x 3.5 cm.
81:3825:1
Gift of A. Ralph Barker

14.
EDWARD S. DUNSHEE
(active 1864–?)
[Unidentified female]
ca. 1864
Ambrotype, applied color
Sixth plate
81:2752:1
Gift of Mrs. John Benjamin

15.
ERASTUS and WALLACE
    DARROW, publisher
(active 1865–?)
[Flood of 1865]
1865
Albumen print
22.7 x 30.3 cm.
83:0098:1
Museum collection

16.
BENJAMIN F. POWELSON (attrib.)
(1823–1885)
[Flood of 1865, street scene]
1865
Albumen print
Carte-de-visite, 9.6 x 5.6 cm.
81:4831:2
Gift of Joan Schild

17.
BENJAMIN F. POWELSON (attrib.)
(1823–1885)
[Flood of 1865]
1865
Albumen print
Carte-de-visite, 5.7 x 7.5 cm.
81:4831:3
Gift of Joan Schild

18.
BENJAMIN F. POWELSON (attrib.)
(1823–1885)
[Flood of 1865]
1865
Albumen print
Carte-de-visite, 8.7 x 5.7 cm.
81:4831:1
Gift of Joan Schild

19.
UNIDENTIFIED PHOTOGRAPHER
[Flood of 1865]
1865
Albumen print
24.0 x 30.5 cm.
83:0088:1
Gift of Mrs. A. Gilman

20.
EDWARD S. DUNSHEE
(active 1864–?)
[Unidentified female]
ca. 1865
Albumen print, applied color
Carte-de-visite, 9.3 x 5.4 cm.
81:3383:2
Gift of A. Ralph Barker

21.
BENJAMIN F. HALE
(1831–1900) (active 1858–ca.
    1897)
[Unidentified woman and child]
ca. 1865
Albumen print
Carte-de-visite, 9.5 x 5.5 cm.
81:3608:1
Gift of A. Ralph Barker

22.
JULIUS J. KEMPE and MENZO E.
    GATES
(active 1864–1865)
"Charles & Marcia H. Seely"
ca. 1865
Albumen print
Carte-de-visite, 9.2 x 5.5 cm.
81:3913:1
Gift of Miss M. Ramsey Harris

23.
MASTERSON & WOOD
(active 1865–1866)
[Genesee River, Upper Falls]
ca. 1865
Albumen print
Carte-de-visite, 5.5 x 8.7 cm.
81:4686:1
Gift of A. Ralph Barker

24.
BENJAMIN F. POWELSON
(1823–1885)
"Ross and Erma Schraft"
ca. 1865
Albumen print
Carte-de-visite, 9.3 x 5.8 cm.
76:0278:9
Gift of William Brown

25.
BENJAMIN F. POWELSON
(1823–1885)
[Unidentified male]
ca. 1865
Albumen print
Carte-de-visite, 9.4 x 5.3 cm.
81:4825:7
Museum collection

26.
BENJAMIN F. POWELSON
(1823–1885)
[Unidentified female child]
ca. 1865
Albumen print
Carte-de-visite, 9.5 x 5.3 cm.
81:4829:4
Museum purchase

27.
BENJAMIN F. POWELSON
(1823–1885)
[Parade scene]
ca. 1865
Albumen print
Carte-de-visite, 9.4 x 5.6 cm.
81:4833:1
Museum collection

LATER CENTURY (1866–1900)

28.
JOHN HOWE KENT
(1827–1910) (active 1865–1910)
"Sprague"
ca. 1866
Albumen print
Carte-de-visite, 9.2 x 5.3 cm.
81:3916:15
Gift of Mrs. Lyndon Wells

29.
SUNBEAM GALLERY; GEORGE
W. GODFREY (attrib.)
(1818–1888) (active 1865–1887)
[Unidentified female child]
ca. 1866-67
Albumen print
Carte-de-visite, 9.2 x 5.5 cm.
70:0184:7
Museum collection

30.
JOHN HOWE KENT
(1827–1910) (active 1865–1910)
[Unidentified females]
ca. 1868-70
Albumen print
Carte-de-visite, 9.3 x 5.8 cm.
81:3924:1
Gift of American Antiquarian
Society

31.
R. H. BLIVEN
(active 1870s)
"Proboscis of House Fly"
ca. 1870s
from: "Wonders of the
Microscope" series
Albumen prints
Stereograph, 8.9 x 16.3 cm.
ensemble
81:6504:2
Museum collection

32.
JOHN HOWE KENT
(1827–1910) (active 1865–1910)
[Unidentified female]
ca. 1870s
Albumen print
Carte-de-visite, 9.7 x 5.9 cm.
81:3920:1
Gift of A. Ralph Barker

33.
JACOB BARHYDT
(1822–1874)
[Unidentified male]
ca. 1872
Albumen print
Carte-de-visite, 9.8 x 5.6 cm.
82:0261:7
Museum collection

34.
JOHN HOWE KENT
(1827–1910) (active 1865–1910)
"Kittie E. Selen"
1875
Albumen print
Carte-de-visite, 9.3 x 5.6 cm.
81:3920:6
Gift of A. Ralph Barker

35.
ELIZABETH C. HEDLEY
(active 1874–1879)
"Helen M. Whipple" or "Annie
Cutler"
ca. 1875
Albumen print
Carte-de-visite, 9.2 x 5.2 cm.
81:3753:1
Museum purchase

36.
GEORGE H. MONROE
(1851–1916) (active 1873–1882)
Bridge to Well, Fountain in
Distance. Rochester Water
Works.
ca. 1875
from: "Artistic Views of Rochester
and its Environs.
The 'Flower City'" series
Albumen prints
Stereograph, 10.3 x 15.3 cm.
ensemble (domed)
79:1636:1
Gift of 3M Co., ex-collection Louis
Walton Sipley

37.
UNIDENTIFIED PHOTOGRAPHER
A. V. Smith Block.-Ernest Hart's
Printing Office
(including John Howe Kent's
studio)
ca. 1875
Albumen prints
Stereograph, 7.8 x 15.0 cm.
ensemble (domed)
81:7591:1
Museum collection

38.
JOHN HOWE KENT
(1827–1910) (active 1865–1910)
[Unidentified female]
ca. 1876
Albumen print
101.9 x 69.8 cm.
77:0834:1
Gift of 3M Co., ex-collection Louis
Walton Sipley

39.
CHARLES WARREN
WOODWARD
(1836–1894) (active as publisher,
1862–1894)
Arnold Park
ca. 1876
from: "American Scenery,
Rochester and Vicinity" series
Albumen prints
Stereograph, 8.0 x 14.9 cm.
ensemble
81:8716:24
Museum purchase

40.
CHARLES WARREN
WOODWARD
(1836–1894) (active as publisher,
1862–1894)
Central Church
ca. 1876
from: "American Scenery,
Rochester and Vicinity" series
Albumen prints
Stereograph, 8.0 x 14.9 cm.
ensemble
81:8716:27
Museum purchase

41.
CHARLES WARREN
WOODWARD
(1836–1894) (active as publisher,
1862–1894)
City Hospital
ca. 1876
from: "American Scenery,
Rochester and Vicinity" series
Albumen prints
Stereograph, 7.9 x 14.9 cm.
ensemble
81:8716:10
Museum purchase

42.
CHARLES WARREN
WOODWARD
(1836–1894) (active as publisher,
1862–1894)
Masonic Hall
ca. 1876
from: "American Scenery,
Rochester and Vicinity" series
Albumen prints
Stereograph, 8.0 x 15.0 cm.
ensemble
81:8716:13
Museum purchase

43.
CHARLES WARREN
WOODWARD
(1836–1894) (active as publisher,
1862–1894)
View from Bank North of Chapel
ca. 1876
from: "American Scenery,
Rochester and Vicinity" series
Albumen prints
Stereograph, 8.0 x 15.0 cm.
ensemble
81:8716:52
Museum purchase

44.
GEORGE W. GODFREY
(1818–1888)
"Ella & Flora Dix"
1880
Albumen print
Cabinet card, 14.2 x 10.1 cm.
83:1819:11
Gift of Merritt Mosher

45.
GEORGE W. GODFREY (attrib.)
(1818–1888)
"Flora & Ella Dix"
1880
Tintype
Sixth plate
76:0049:9
Gift of Merritt Mosher

46.
R. H. WALDRON
(active 1880–1881)
[Unidentified female]
1880
Albumen print
Carte-de-visite, 9.0 x 5.7 cm.
81:5440:1
Museum collection

47.
UNIDENTIFIED PHOTOGRAPHER
[Genesee River, Generator station
at Lower Falls]
ca. 1880
Albumen print
11.8 x 16.3 cm.
83:0065:47
Gift of Franklin W. Judson

48.
UNIDENTIFIED PHOTOGRAPHER
[Genesee River Gorge]
ca. 1880
Albumen print
12.0 x 16.5 cm.
83:0065:48
Gift of Franklin W. Judson

49.
UNIDENTIFIED PHOTOGRAPHER
[Genesee River, Lower Falls,
   Rochester, New York]
ca. 1880s
Albumen print
11.8 x 17.0 cm.
83:0108:1
Gift of Mrs. David L. Bell

50.
LEVI SHERMAN
(1834–1901) (active 1874–1896)
[Unidentified child]
ca. 1880s
Gelatin silver print
Cabinet card, 14.9 x 9.7 cm.
81:4115:1
Gift of Walter Schoeneman

51.
CHARLES T. POMEROY
(active 1878–1886)
[Unidentified male]
1882
Albumen print
Cabinet card, 14.9 x 9.8 cm.
82:1296:1
Gift of E. J. Ward

52.
CHARLES T. POMEROY
(active 1878–1886)
[Unidentified female children in
   studio prop boat]
ca. 1882-84
Albumen print
Cabinet card, 15.0 x 9.8 cm.
81:4000:4
Museum collection

53.
JOHN E. DUMONT
(active 1880s & 1890s)
Listening to the Birds
1885
Photogravure print
29.5 x 23.7 cm.
80:0131:2
Gift of Dr. & Mrs. E. Hoffman

54.
JOHN WILSON TAYLOR
(active 1874–1916)
[Man with bicycle]
ca. 1885
Albumen print
Cabinet card, 14.1 x 9.9 cm.
81:4178:6
Museum collection

55.
WARDLAW and LEARNED
(active 1884–1886)
[Unidentified female]
ca. 1885
Albumen print
Cabinet card, 15.2 x 10.1 cm.
69:0112:9
Gift of Mrs. Paul A. Favieu

56.
CHARLES T. POMEROY
(active 1878–1886)
[Funerary floral arrangement with
   photograph]
1886
Albumen print
Cabinet card, 9.9 x 14.0 cm.
81:4000:1
Museum collection

57.
UNIDENTIFIED PHOTOGRAPHER
"Ella Dix Mosher with Florence
   and Marion Mosher"
ca. 1888
Tintype, applied color
Sixth plate
76:0049:6
Gift of Merritt Mosher

58.
A. E. DUMBLE
(active 1874–1896)
"Amy Busby"
1889
Albumen print
Cabinet card, 14.5 x 9.9 cm.
82:0784:1
Gift of G. L. Howe

59.
UNIDENTIFIED PHOTOGRAPHER
[Genesee River, Lower Falls and
   Bridge]
1890
Transparency, glass
Lantern slide, 5.8 x 7.1 cm.
83:0200:7
Museum collection

60.
UNIDENTIFIED PHOTOGRAPHER (S)
Rochester Illustrated, (12 parts),
   Rochester, H. R. Page & Co.
1890
Serial publication, illustrated with
   photomechanical reproductions
35.1 x 28.1 cm. (issue size)
RB F 129 R7
Museum collection

61.
UNIDENTIFIED PHOTOGRAPHER
"Fanny Dix Brown, Hattie Geer,
   Flora Dix Proctor, seated"
ca. 1890
Tintype
Sixth plate
76:0049:11
Gift of Merritt Mosher

62.
UNIDENTIFIED PHOTOGRAPHER
"Flora Dix Proctor, Marion Dix
   Mosher, Florence E. Mosher,
   Mother Ella Dix Mosher"
ca. 1890
Tintype
Sixth plate
76:0049:7
Gift of Merritt Mosher

63.
UNIDENTIFIED PHOTOGRAPHER
[Genesee River and Glen House,
   Lower Falls]
ca. 1890
Gelatin silver print
25.5 x 34.6 cm.
83:0087:1
Museum collection

64.
UNIDENTIFIED PHOTOGRAPHER
[H. H. Warner House]
ca. 1890
Albumen print
28.0 x 18.3 cm.
83:0085:1
Gift of Edna Kitchner

65.
UNIDENTIFIED PHOTOGRAPHER
[Memorial Pavilion, Highland
   Park]
ca. 1890
Gelatin silver print
Kodak # 4 snapshot, 9.8 x 11.9
   cm.
82:2710:5
Gift of Deborah Ritter

66.
UNIDENTIFIED PHOTOGRAPHER
[Old City Hall, Broad Street]
ca. 1890
Gelatin silver print
21.6 x 16.6 cm.
83:0068:1
Gift of Franklin W. Judson

67.
UNIDENTIFIED PHOTOGRAPHER
[Wilder Building]
ca. 1890
Gelatin silver print
21.7 x 16.5 cm.
83:0065:43
Gift of Franklin W. Judson

68.
UNIDENTIFIED PHOTOGRAPHER
[Court House and Old City Hall]
ca. 1890-1900
Transparency, glass
Lantern slide, 7.3 x 10.0 cm.
83:0200:8
Museum collection

69.
UNIDENTIFIED PHOTOGRAPHER
[Erie Canal Aqueduct over
   Genesee River]
ca. 1890-1900
Transparency, glass
Lantern slide, 7.9 x 8.9 cm.
83:0200:11
Museum collection

70.
UNIDENTIFIED PHOTOGRAPHER
[Genesee River near Lake
   Ontario]
ca. 1890-1900
Transparency, glass
Lantern slide, 7.2 x 9.5 cm.
83:0200:10
Museum collection

71.
UNIDENTIFIED PHOTOGRAPHER
[Old City Hall]
ca. 1890-1900
Transparency, glass
Lantern slide, 7.5 x 6.2 cm.
83:0200:1
Museum collection

72.
UNIDENTIFIED PHOTOGRAPHER
[Unidentified canal or river view]
ca. 1890-1900
Transparency, glass
Lantern slide, 7.1 x 9.1 cm.
83:0200:4
Museum collection

73.
CARRIE H. TALCOTT
(amateur, active 1890s)
"Edmund Westervelt" [and
   unidentified companion]
ca. 1892
Gelatin silver print
Kodak # 4 snapshot, 11.8 x 9.5
   cm.
82:1800:1
Gift of Caroline Remington

74.
JOHN WILSON TAYLOR
(active 1874–1916)
[Unidentified children]
ca. 1892-93
Gelatin silver print, applied color
Cabinet card, 14.8 x 10.2 cm.
81:4176:2
Gift of A. Ralph Barker

75.
JOHN E. DUMONT
(active 1880s & 1890s)
"The Columbus Fleet Entering
   Charlotte enroute to Columbian
   Exposition"
1893
Photogravure print
12.9 x 16.9 cm.
80:0128:2
Gift of Ivan Somerville

76.
WILLIS GAYLORD MITCHELL
(active 1890s)
[Sangster's Grocery Store]
1893 (negative)
Modern gelatin silver print from
    original negative
19.3 x 15.6 cm.
83:0149:1MP
Museum collection

77.
JOHN HOWE KENT
(1827–1910) (active 1865–1910)
[Mary & Susan B. Anthony]
ca. 1897
Gelatin silver print
Cabinet card, 14.8 x 10.8 cm.
76:0049:18
Gift of Merritt Mosher

78.
J. ERNEST MOCK
(1868–1944)
[William Storandt]
ca. 1900
Gelatin silver print on glass, hand
    applied color on verso
23.0 x 18.4 cm.
81:0933:2
Gift of Rev. Robert Downs

79.
CHARLES WEBSTER and
    JOSEPHUS ALBEE
(active 1886–1910)
Calling on a Friend
ca. 1900
Gelatin silver prints
Stereograph, 8.0 x 5.2 cm.
    ensemble (domed)
81:8611:26
Gift of J. W. Robson

80.
CHARLES WEBSTER and
    JOSEPHUS ALBEE
(active 1886–1910)
Man in the Moon, Can...
ca. 1900
Gelatin silver prints
Stereograph, 7.6 x 14.9 cm.
    ensemble
81:8611:6
Gift of J. W. Robson

81.
CHARLES WEBSTER and
    JOSEPHUS ALBEE
(active 1886–1910)
Pay Your Money, Take Your
    Choice
ca. 1900
Gelatin silver prints
Stereograph, 7.3 x 15.1 cm.
    ensemble
81:8611:16
Gift of J. W. Robson

82.
UNIDENTIFIED PHOTOGRAPHER
[Erie Canal Aqueduct over
    Genesee River]
ca. 1900
Gelatin silver print
15.7 x 21.4 cm.
83:0065:46
Gift of Franklin W. Judson

EARLY MODERNISM
(1901–1952)

83.
SMITH & CURRY
(active 1900–?)
"Marion J. Wilder"
1902
Gelatin silver print
Cabinet card, 8.9 x 6.2 cm. oval
    (image)
74:0147:83
Gift of Constance D. Taylor

84.
HARRY COUTANT
(active early 1900s)
[Sailboats]
ca. 1903
from: The Bausch and Lomb
    Lens Souvenir, Rochester,
    Bausch & Lomb Optical Co.,
    1903.
Gelatin silver print
7.7 x 10.2 cm.
Museum collection

85.
FRANK GILFUS
(active early 1900s)
[Sibley fire]
1904
Gelatin silver print
20.4 x 15.5 cm.
83:0086:2
Museum collection

86.
RICHARD R. BOZARD
(active 1905–1911)
[Unidentified men at railroad
    tracks]
ca. 1905–1910
Gelatin silver print
12.4 x 17.0 cm.
83:0939:1
Gift of Mrs. Charles Carruth

87.
FREDERICK W. BREHM
(1871–1950)
[Kodak group portrait]
ca. 1910
Gelatin silver print
24.3 x 179.0 cm.
83:0894:1
Museum collection

88.
FREDERICK W. BREHM
(1871–1950)
[Rochester cityscape]
ca. 1910
Gelatin silver print
24.5 x 138.0 cm.
76:0152:3
Museum collection

89.
FREDERICK W. BREHM (attrib.)
(1871–1950)
[Cows, group portrait]
ca. 1910
Gelatin silver print
33.5 x 72.0 cm.
74:0057:65
Gift of John Gibson

90.
JOHN N. HEBERGER
(active ca. 1910–1920)
[Fishing trip]
ca. 1910
Bromide print on fabric
8.0 x 13.0 cm., each
83:0935:1
Gift of the photographer

91.
UNIDENTIFIED PHOTOGRAPHER
[Cutler Building, East Avenue]
ca. 1910-1915
Gelatin silver print
24.6 x 19.0 cm.
75:0134:5
Gift of Mrs. Coddington

92.
JOHN GEORGE CAPSTAFF
    (attrib.)
(1879–1959)
[Unidentified female]
ca. 1915
Reproduction transparency, 1984,
    by Michael Hager, from original
    2 color Kodachrome
23.4 x 18.4 cm.
83:2351:1FP
Gift of Eastman Kodak Company

93.
JOHN GEORGE CAPSTAFF
    (attrib.)
(1879–1959)
[Kodak Park guide, Mr. Strutt]
1915
Reproduction transparency, 1984,
    by Michael Hager, from original
    2 color Kodachrome
19.5 x 14.6 cm.
78:0385:10FP
Gift of Eastman Kodak Company

94.
JOHN GEORGE CAPSTAFF
    (attrib.)
(1879–1959)
[Unidentified male with laboratory
    equipment]
ca. 1915
Reproduction transparency, 1984,
    by Michael Hager, from original
    2 color Kodachrome
23.0 x 18.0 cm.
83:2351:2FP
Gift of Eastman Kodak Company

95.
JOHN GEORGE CAPSTAFF
    (attrib.)
(1879–1959)
[Unidentified male with
    photograph]
ca. 1915
Reproduction transparency, 1984,
    by Michael Hager, from original
    2 color Kodachrome
23.9 x 18.8 cm.
83:2351:3FP
Gift of Eastman Kodak Company

96.
UNIDENTIFIED PHOTOGRAPHER
"Camera Goes Abroad"
1918
from: U. S. A. School of Aerial
    Photography, Rochester, NY,
    1918.
Gelatin silver print
19.0 x 24.5 cm.
81:1702:56
Gift of Dwight R. Furness

97.
UNIDENTIFIED PHOTOGRAPHER
"Illustrated Lectures are an
    Important Part of Instruction"
1918
from: U. S. A. School of Aerial
    Photography, Rochester, NY,
    1918.
Gelatin silver print
19.0 x 24.5 cm.
81:1702:18
Gift of Dwight R. Furness

98.
UNIDENTIFIED PHOTOGRAPHER
"Somewhere Over Rochester,
    Observer and Pilot at Work"
1918
from: U. S. A. School of Aerial
    Photography, Rochester, NY,
    1918.
Gelatin silver print
18.8 x 24.4 cm.
81:1702:57
Gift of Dwight R. Furness

99.
A. W. STEVENS
[Aerial mosaic of Rochester]
1920
Gelatin silver print
48.0 x 38.0 cm.
83:2526:1
Gift of Dr. Walter Clark

100.
FREDERICK C. MOSER
(active ca. 1915–1942)
[Dancer from Denio Civic Ballet]
ca. 1920s
Gelatin silver print, applied color
16.9 x 22.6 cm.
L83:0558:4
Lent by a private collection

101.
CHARLES ZOLLER
(1854–1934)
[Eastman Kodak parade float]
ca. 1920s
Reproduction transparency, 1984,
    by Michael Hager, from screen
    (Autochrome) glass plate
6.7 x 8.4 cm.
79:4268:1FP
Museum collection, ex-Zoller
    Collection

102.
CHARLES ZOLLER
(1854–1934)
[St. Paul's Episcopal Church]
ca. 1920s
Reproduction transparency, 1984,
    by Michael Hager, from screen
    (Autochrome) glass plate
7.1 x 7.3 cm.
82:2087:1FP
Museum collection, ex-Zoller
    Collection

103.
UNIDENTIFIED PHOTOGRAPHER
[School children, School # 40,
    Dewey Avenue]
ca. 1923
Gelatin silver print
19.0 x 24.4 cm.
82:2612:3
Gift of Viola Sherman

104.
CHARLES ZOLLER
(1854–1934)
[Rochester at night]
1927
Reproduction transparency, 1984,
    by Michael Hager, from screen
    (Autochrome) glass plate
7.3 x 9.0 cm.
82:2041:1FP
Museum collection, ex-Zoller
    Collection

105.
ALEXANDER LEVENTON
(1895–1950)
Frantisek Drtikol
1930
Gelatin silver print
24.2 x 18.5 cm.
83:2419:8
Gift of Mrs. Alexander Leventon

106.
EUGENE P. WIGHTMAN
(?–1979)
Alexander Leventon
ca. 1930
Chlorobromide print
27.0 x 22.1 cm.
76:0194:7
Gift of the photographer

107.
CHARLES M. ROWE
(1873–1946)
[Three sequential views of the
    construction of Monroe
    Community Hospital]
1931-1932
Gelatin silver prints (3)
7.7 x 48.9 cm. (each print)
L84:0060:1, 2, 3
Lent by Richard M. Rowe

108.
GLENN E. MATTHEWS
(1897–   )
Industrial Building-Rochester
    Centennial Exposition
1934
Gelatin silver print
18.6 x 14.5 cm.
79:1828:27
Gift of the photographer

109.
ARTHUR W. FUCHS
(1907–?)
"Stein-Female"
ca. 1934
Gelatin silver radiograph (x-ray)
180.0 x 79.0 cm.
L84:0047:1
Lent by Eastman Kodak Company

110.
WALTER CLARK
British (1899–   )
[Leopold Godowsky, Jr. and
    Leopold Mannes, inventors of
    the Kodachrome process]
1938
Dye imbibition (Eastman Wash-off
    Relief) print, ca.1940, by Louis
    Condax, from chromogenic
    development (Kodachrome)
    transparency
27.2 x 39.4 cm.
79:4196:1
Gift of Dr. Walter Clark

111.
LOUIS CONDAX
(1896–1971)
[Vivien Leigh]
ca. 1939
Dye imbibition (Kodak Dye
    Transfer) print
36.8 x 32.3 cm.
80:0783:2
Gift of Philip Condax

112.
LOUIS OUZER
(1913–   )
Joan
ca. late 1940s
Gelatin silver print
40.0 x 50.0 cm.
L84:0063:1
Lent by the photographer

113.
EUGENE P. WIGHTMAN
(?–1979)
After the Swim
ca. 1949
Gelatin silver print
25.7 x 32.0 cm.
76:0194:5
Gift of the photographer

114.
JEANETTE KLUTE
(1918–   )
[Landscape]
ca. 1950
Dye imbibition (Kodak Dye
    Transfer) print
31.9 x 24.1 cm.
81:1291:39
On permanent loan from Eastman
    Kodak Company

115.
ANSEL E. ADAMS
(1902–1984)
[View of Rochester, NY]
1952
Gelatin silver print
24.1 x 31.7 cm.
L83:2323:2
Courtesy of Andrew D. Wolfe

THE AGE OF PHOTOGRAPHIC EDUCATION (1953–PRESENT)

116.
MINOR WHITE
(1908–1976)
Black Sun
1955
from: "Sequence 10", 1955
Gelatin silver print
18.7 x 21.0 cm.
81:2301:1
Gift of the photographer

117.
WALTER CHAPPELL
(1925–   )
Gestures of Infinity
1957
Artist's book, illustrated with
    gelatin silver prints
29.2 x 36.5 cm. (publication size)
Museum collection

118.
MINOR WHITE
(1908–1976)
Windowsill Daydreaming
1958
Gelatin silver print
22.5 x 18.0 cm.
77:0369:105
Museum collection

119.
HOWARD J. ROWE
(1910–   )
[Giant gear, Farrel Corporation]
ca. late 1950s
Gelatin silver print
39.2 x 49.2 cm.
L84:0060:4
Lent by Richard M. Rowe

120.
ROBERT W. FICHTER
(1939–   )
[Dianagram]
1967
Gelatin silver print
23.5 x 34.7 cm.
67:0112:5
Museum purchase

121.
NATHAN LYONS
(1930–   )
Untitled
1968, 1969/82
from: "Notations in Passing"
    series,
from: Victor Landweber (ed.),
    American Roads, Los Angeles,
    Landweber/Artists, 1982, plate
    # 13.
Gelatin silver prints
11.4 x 17.0 cm., each (diptych)
83:2321:13
Museum purchase, Lila Acheson
    Wallace Fund

122.
THOMAS F. BARROW
(1938–   )
Homage to J. Wright
1969
Gelatin silver print, toned
22.7 x 33.5 cm.
70:0167:4
Museum purchase

123.
MICHAEL BISHOP
(1946–   )
Untitled
1969
Gelatin silver prints
14.9 x 14.9 cm. (left), 14.8 x 14.9
    cm. (right), diptych
70:0173:1
Museum purchase

124.
HAROLD H. JONES
(1940–   )
Cadillac, 1969
1969
from: "untitled poems to the sky"
    series
Gelatin silver print, applied color
14.9 x 14.8 cm.
73:0065:2
Museum collection, by exchange

125.
LES KRIMS
(1943–   )
[Interior view, people with balloon]
1969
Gelatin silver print
13.1 x 19.2 cm.
78:0516:11
Museum collection

126.
KEITH SMITH
(1938–   )
[Self portrait]
1970
Silkscreen on fabric
180.0 x 165.0 cm. (quilt), 23.3 x
    32.8 cm. (each image)
71:0014:1
Museum purchase

127.
BETTY HAHN
(1940–   )
[Kinescopes in George Eastman
    House]
1971
Gum-bichromate on fabric
28.5 x 35.7 cm.
77:0054:1
Gift of the photographer

128.
ROGER MERTIN
(1942–   )
Rochester, N. Y.
1973
Gelatin silver print
20.8 x 31.2 cm.
74:0124:1
Museum purchase, National
    Endowment for the Arts

129.
BEA NETTLES
(1946–   )
The Imaginary Blowtorch
1973
Artist's book, various processes
26.5 x 20.8 cm. (publication size)
Museum collection

130.
VISUAL STUDIES WORKSHOP
1974 Portfolio Project,
Rochester, Visual Studies
    Workshop, 1974.
Portfolio, various processes
35.0 x 28.0 cm. (publication size)
79:0216:1-37
Gift of the Visual Studies
    Workshop

131.
JOE DEAL
(1947–   )
Along I-490 (Rochester)
1975
Gelatin silver print
32.4 x 32.4 cm.
78:1127:2
Museum purchase

132.
ROCHESTER INSTITUTE OF
    TECHNOLOGY
MFA Photography Program
    PORTFOLIO 75, Rochester,
    Rochester Institute of
    Technology, 1975.
Portfolio, various processes
35.0 x 28.0 cm.
78:0638:1-30
Museum purchase

133.
LANDSAT SATELLITE
Color Aerial View of Rochester,
    N. Y.
ca. 1975
Chromogenic development
    (Ektacolor) print
38.1 x 38.1 cm.
78:0048:2
Gift of Dr. Wesley Hanson

134.
CHARLES A. ARNOLD
(1922–   )
[Still life]
1978
from: MFA Photography Program,
    PORTFOLIO VI, Rochester,
    Rochester Institute of
    Technology, 1978.
Xerographic reproduction
16.9 x 20.4 cm.
78:0784:1
Museum purchase

135.
RICK MCKEE HOCK
(1947–   )
View from Court Street Bridge,
    Genesee River, looking south
1978
Gelatin silver print
19.5 x 24.5 cm.
83:2335:3
Gift of the photographer

136.
RICHARD MARGOLIS
(1943–   )
156, Rochester
1978
Gelatin silver print, toned
21.4 x 31.1 cm.
79:1785:3
Museum purchase

137.
JOHN PFAHL
(1939–   )
31 Prince Street, Rochester, New
    York
1978
Chromogenic development
    (Ektacolor) print
40.5 x 50.7 cm.
81:3207:8
Gift of Robert Friedus

138.
BRUCE DAVID HOROWITZ
(1949–   )
Untitled
1980
Gelatin silver print
34.8 x 34.8 cm.
L83:1818:1
Lent by the photographer

139.
JOAN LYONS
(1937–   )
[Female portrait]
1980
from; Joan Lyons, PRESENCES,
    Rochester, Visual Studies
    Workshop Press, 1980.
Offset photo lithographic print
54.3 x 42.3 cm.
81:2811:3
Museum purchase, Intrepid Fund
    and National Endowment for
    the Arts

140.
TIM J. CALLAHAN
(1956–   )
Untitled # 10
1981
Dye imbibition (Kodak Dye
    Transfer) print
19.1 x 24.0 cm.
L83:1221:1
Lent by the photographer

141.
JANE ALDEN STEVENS
(1952–   )
Untitled # 4
1981
Gelatin silver print on aluminum
29.4 x 47.7 cm.
L83:1222:1
Lent by the photographer

142.
RICHARD M. ROWE
(1948–   )
[Sonic detection system,
    Detection Systems, Inc.]
ca. 1981
Gelatin silver print
25.7 x 18.0 cm.
L84:0060:5
Lent by the photographer

143.
LAWRENCE MERRILL
(1948–   )
Rochester, N. Y.
1982
Chromogenic development
    (Ektacolor) print
20.4 x 20.4 cm.
82:2616:3
Museum purchase, Intrepid Fund
    and National Endowment for
    the Arts

144.
TED KAWALERSKI
(1948–   )
Allen Neuharth
1982/1983
Cibachrome print, 34.3 x 22.5 cm.
L83:2149:1
Lent by the photographer

145.
DOUGLAS BEUBE
(1950–   )
Matches
1983
Artist's book, illustrated with
    gelatin silver prints in mixed
    media constructed box
25.4 x 16.0 cm. (book); 41.3 x
    28.5 cm. (box)
L83:2103:1
Lent by the photographer

146.
MARILYN BRIDGES
(1948–   )
Farmhouse, Le Roy, NY
1983
Gelatin silver print, toned
38.0 x 47.8 cm.
L83:2123:4
Lent by the photographer

147.
GUENTHER CARTWRIGHT
(1945–)
West Henrietta, New York
1983
Chromogenic development
   (Ektacolor) print
25.0 x 38.0 cm.
L83:2528:1
Lent by the photographer

148.
LESLIE KIPPEN
(1949–)
"Overview of Convention Center
   Site"
1983
Chromogenic development
   (Ektacolor) print
27.2 x 34.9 cm.
L83:1513:1
Lent by the photographer

149.
ANNE LENNOX
(1944–)
Black Cashmere with Boa
1983
Cibachrome print from original
   Kodachrome transparency
49.8 x 34.0 cm.
84:0076:1
Gift of the photographer, courtesy
   Gannett Rochester Newspapers

150.
CHARLOTTE QUEHL
(1948–)
First Federal Building
1983
Cibachrome print
31.4 x 26.0 cm.
L83:1514:1
Lent by the photographer

151.
JOSEPH VITONE
(1954–)
Untitled
1983
Chromogenic development
   (Ektacolor) print
38.1 x 48.3 cm.
L83:1515:1
Lent by the photographer

152.
UNIDENTIFIED PHOTOGRAPHER
[George Eastman, Age 3]
ca. 1857
Tintype
Sixteenth plate
83:2007:1
Gift of Eastman Kodak Company

153.
UNIDENTIFIED PHOTOGRAPHER
[George Eastman]
ca. 1868
Tintype
Quarter plate
79:2962:1
Museum collection

154.
GEORGE EASTMAN
(1854–1932)
[Genesee River]
1877
Ambrotype
Half plate
83:2014:1
Gift of George Dryden

155.
GEORGE EASTMAN
(1854–1932)
[Ledger Sheets for
   October-December]
1877
Manuscript
22.5 x 21.4 cm.; 26.7 x 21.5 cm.
83:2021:1-2
Museum collection

156.
GEORGE EASTMAN
(1854–1932)
[Mr. Nadar, Place de L'Opéra,
   Paris]
1890
Gelatin silver print
Kodak # 2 snapshot, 9.1 cm.
   diameter
81:1159:27
Gift of Margaret Weston

157.
GEORGE EASTMAN
(1854–1932)
[Vest pocket memo book of
   addresses and expenses]
1890
Manuscript
9.8 x 5.3 cm.
79:2957:1
Museum collection

158.
GEORGE EASTMAN (attrib.)
(1854–1932)
[Charles P. Ham House]
1880
Albumen print (?)
11.9 x 9.8 cm.
83:2008:1
Museum collection

159.
NADAR (GASPARD FÉLIX
   TOURNACHON)
French (1820–1910)
[George Eastman]
1890
Albumen print
Boudoir card, 19.6 x 12.5 cm.
81:4547:1
Gift of George Dryden

160.
FREDERICK FARGO CHURCH
(1864–1925)
[George Eastman]
1892
Albumen print
Kodak # 2 snapshot, 9.1 cm.
   diameter
81:1159:26
Gift of Margaret Weston

161.
GEORGE EASTMAN
(1854–1932)
A Dinner; Saturday evening,
   October Seventh, 1905, given
   by Mr. George Eastman,
   Buffalo, Matthews-Northrup
   Works, 1905.
1905
Book, illustrated with 16 gravures
18.0 x 9.2 cm.
RB TX 728 E25
Museum collection

162.
ALMAN & CO.
(active ca. 1910–1920)
[George Eastman]
ca. 1915
Gelatin silver print
53.1 x 42.7 cm.
83:0041:1
Museum collection

163.
GEORGE EASTMAN
(1854–1932)
Chronicles of an African Trip,
   Rochester, privately
   printed for the author.
1927
Book, illustrated with 53 leaves of
   plates
24.5 x 15.8 cm.
RB TR 140 E27
Museum collection

164.
UNIDENTIFIED PHOTOGRAPHER
[Safari to Kenya, Eastman carried
   by bearers]
1927-28
Gelatin silver print
26.7 x 34.2 cm.
83:2406:2
Museum collection

165.
UNIDENTIFIED PHOTOGRAPHER
[Safari to Kenya, Eastman with
   Elephant]
1927-28
Gelatin silver print
26.7 x 34.2 cm.
83:2406:1
Museum collection

166.
LUBOSHEZ (photographer)
(active 1920s)
[United States postage stamp
   honoring George Eastman]
1954
Photomechanical reproduction
   from original photograph of
   1927
2.3 x 2.0 cm. (each stamp)
83:2009:1
Museum collection

167.
LUBOSHEZ (photographer)
(active 1920s)
[Official First Day Cover
   "Honoring George Eastman"]
1954
Photomechanical reproduction
   from original photograph of
   1927
3.9 x 2.9 cm. (image)
83:2009:2
Museum collection

168.
IRVING POBBORAVSKY
(1933–)
[International Museum of
   Photography at George
   Eastman House]
1973
Daguerreotype
Whole plate
81:1807:1
Gift of Rochester Photographic
   Historical Society

169.
DEL ZOGG
(1947–)
"In George's Garden, 1983"
1983
from: "In George's Garden"
   series
Chromogenic development
   (Ektacolor) print
19.1 x 19.3 cm.
L83:2400:1
Lent by the photographer

170.
GEORGE EASTMAN
(1854–1932)
Weekly Time Book,
   March-December 1881
1881
Manuscript
17.0 x 11.8 cm.
79:2952:1
Museum collection

171.
UNIDENTIFIED PHOTOGRAPHER
"House of Seven Gables, Salem,
 Mass."
1888
Gelatin silver print
Kodak # 1 snapshot, 6.7 cm.
 diameter
81:1294:162
Museum collection

172.
UNIDENTIFIED PHOTOGRAPHER
"Old Houses-Salem, Mass."
1888
Gelatin silver print
Kodak # 1 snapshot, 6.7 cm.
 diameter
81:1294:161
Museum collection

173.
EASTMAN KODAK COMPANY
(active 1881–)
The Kodak Manual. (Typescript
 with notations by George
 Eastman) Rochester, Eastman
 Dry Plate and Film Co.
ca. 1888
Typescript, 15 pages
33.0 x 21.5 cm.
79:2950:1
Museum collection

174.
EASTMAN KODAK COMPANY
(active 1881–)
The Kodak Manual. Rochester,
 Eastman Dry Plate and Film Co.
1889
Book, 76 p. ill.
17.0 x 12.7 cm.
RB TR 263 K6 E23 1889d
Museum collection

175.
UNIDENTIFIED PHOTOGRAPHER
"Marion Howland, Easthampton,
 Mass."
1890
Gelatin silver print
Kodak # 2 snapshot, 9.1 cm.
 diameter
81:2603:89
Gift of Greene County Historical
 Society

176.
ALBERT B. EASTWOOD
(1867–1958)
"Bridal Veil Falls in Yosemite"
ca. 1890s
Gelatin silver print
Kodak # 4 snapshot, 11.5 x 9.3
 cm.
82:1798:38
Museum collection

177.
ALBERT B. EASTWOOD
(1867–1958)
"From Verandah of Hotel in the
 Valley"
ca. 1890s
Gelatin silver print
Kodak # 4 snapshot, 11.7 x 9.2
 cm.
82:1798:37
Museum collection

178.
ALBERT B. EASTWOOD
(1867–1958)
"Glimpse into the valley from
 Inspiration Point"
ca. 1890s
Gelatin silver print
Kodak # 4 snapshot, 11.7 x 9.4
 cm.
82:1798:62
Museum collection

179.
ALBERT B. EASTWOOD
(1867–1958)
"Yosemite-falls 2600 ft high"
ca. 1890s
Gelatin silver print
Kodak # 4 snapshot, 11.6 x 9.4
 cm.
82:1798:36
Museum collection

180.
UNIDENTIFIED PHOTOGRAPHER
"Awfully Good"
ca. 1890s
Gelatin silver print
Kodak # 2 snapshot, 9.1 cm.
 diameter
81:2167:113
Gift of George B. Dryden

181.
UNIDENTIFIED PHOTOGRAPHER
"Descending Vesuvius"
ca. 1890s
Gelatin silver print
Kodak # 1 snapshot, 6.7 cm.
 diameter
74:0250:48
Gift of Mrs. Raymond Albright

182.
UNIDENTIFIED PHOTOGRAPHER
"Dixie"
ca. 1890s
Gelatin silver print
Kodak # 1 snapshot, 6.2 cm.
 diameter
74:0245:53
Gift of Mrs. Raymond Albright

183.
UNIDENTIFIED PHOTOGRAPHER
"4th July Tournament"
ca. 1890s
Gelatin silver print
Kodak # 2 snapshot, 9.2 cm.
 diameter
81:2167:92
Gift of George B. Dryden

184.
UNIDENTIFIED PHOTOGRAPHER
"Head of statue at Ramesseum,
 Thebes. Ruth at side"
ca. 1890s
Gelatin silver print
Kodak # 1 snapshot, 6.2 cm.
 diameter
74:0253:26
Gift of Mrs. Raymond Albright

185.
UNIDENTIFIED PHOTOGRAPHER
"Helen Taylor"
ca. 1890s
Gelatin silver print
Kodak # 3 snapshot, 8.4 x 9.3 cm.
82:3133:16
Gift of Dennis Atkinson

186.
UNIDENTIFIED PHOTOGRAPHER
"Interesting"
ca. 1890s
Gelatin silver print
Kodak # 2 snapshot, 9.2 cm.
 diameter
81:2167:104
Gift of George B. Dryden

187.
UNIDENTIFIED PHOTOGRAPHER
"Interior of Erechtheum,
 Acropolis, Athens"
ca. 1890s
Gelatin silver print
Kodak # 1 snapshot, 6.7 cm.
 diameter
74:0250:11
Gift of Mrs. Raymond Albright

188.
UNIDENTIFIED PHOTOGRAPHER
"Kodak's First Picnic"
ca. 1890s
Gelatin silver print
Kodak # 4 snapshot, 9.7 x 11.7
 cm.
75:0038:13
Museum collection

189.
UNIDENTIFIED PHOTOGRAPHER
"Libbie Wegman, Minnie Hoefler"
ca. 1890s
Gelatin silver print
Kodak # 1 snapshot, 6.4 cm.
 diameter
81:1294:110
Museum collection

190.
UNIDENTIFIED PHOTOGRAPHER
"London Street from top
 Omnibus"
ca. 1890s
Gelatin silver print
Kodak # 1 snapshot, 6.2 cm.
 diameter
74:0246:34
Gift of Mrs. Raymond Albright

191.
UNIDENTIFIED PHOTOGRAPHER
"Love in a cottage"
ca. 1890s
Gelatin silver print
Kodak # 2 snapshot, 9.2 cm.
 diameter
81:2167:88
Gift of George B. Dryden

192.
UNIDENTIFIED PHOTOGRAPHER
"Mama and the kid"
ca. 1890s
Gelatin silver print
Kodak # 2 snapshot, 9.2 cm.
 diameter
81:2167:135
Gift of George B. Dryden

193.
UNIDENTIFIED PHOTOGRAPHER
"Minnie Hoefler"
ca. 1890s
Gelatin silver print
Kodak # 4 snapshot, 12.5 x 10.2
 cm.
82:1801:13
Museum collection

194.
UNIDENTIFIED PHOTOGRAPHER
"Miss L. Daniels, Miss Dintrup,
 Miss H. Stone, Minnie Hoefler,
 Frank Sprague, Ella Hrudieus,
 Mattie Arnold, Cora Spinning,
 Edith Walenhaupt"
ca. 1890s
Gelatin silver print
Kodak # 2 snapshot, 9.3 cm.
 diameter
81:2862:50
Museum collection

195.
UNIDENTIFIED PHOTOGRAPHER
"Pierre Ditto"
ca. 1890s
Gelatin silver print
Kodak # 2 snapshot, 9.3 cm.
 diameter
81:2167:133
Gift of George B. Dryden

196.
UNIDENTIFIED PHOTOGRAPHER
"Queen of Greece in Carriage,
 Athens"
ca. 1890s
Gelatin silver print
Kodak # 1 snapshot, 6.4 cm.
 diameter
74:0252:83
Gift of Mrs. Raymond Albright

197.
UNIDENTIFIED PHOTOGRAPHER
"Sherman Barris, Minnie Hoefler,
  Cora Harvey, Bell Baker" [and
  others]
ca. 1890s
Gelatin silver print
Kodak # 2 snapshot, 9.2 cm.
  diameter
81:2862:49
Museum collection

198.
UNIDENTIFIED PHOTOGRAPHER
"Staged railroad collision"
ca. 1890s
Gelatin silver print
Kodak # 1 snapshot, 6.2 cm.
  diameter
81:1294:187
Museum collection

199.
UNIDENTIFIED PHOTOGRAPHER
"Temple Bar, London"
ca. 1890s
Gelatin silver print
Kodak # 1 snapshot, 6.2 cm.
  diameter
74:0246:35
Gift of Mrs. Raymond Albright

200.
UNIDENTIFIED PHOTOGRAPHER
"Umbria"
ca. 1890s
Gelatin silver print
Kodak # 1 snapshot, 6.2 cm.
  diameter
74:0246:6
Gift of Mrs. Raymond Albright

201.
UNIDENTIFIED PHOTOGRAPHER
[Boys with ladder]
ca. 1890s
Gelatin silver print
Kodak # 2 snapshot, 9.1 cm.
  diameter
81:2603:102
Gift of Greene County Historical
  Society

202.
UNIDENTIFIED PHOTOGRAPHER
[Boys on porch]
ca. 1890s
Gelatin silver print
Kodak # 1 snapshot, 6.4 cm.
  diameter
81:1154:50
Ex-collection Alden Scott Boyer

203.
UNIDENTIFIED PHOTOGRAPHER
[Boy in rocking chair]
ca. 1890s
Gelatin silver print
Kodak # 1 snapshot, 6.4 cm.
  diameter
74:0245:18
Gift of Mrs. Raymond Albright

204.
UNIDENTIFIED PHOTOGRAPHER
[Cow and fence]
ca. 1890s
Gelatin silver print
Kodak # 1 snapshot, 6.3 cm.
  diameter
74:0245:9
Gift of Mrs. Raymond Albright

205.
UNIDENTIFIED PHOTOGRAPHER
[Double exposure]
ca. 1890s
Gelatin silver print
Kodak # 1 snapshot, 6.2 cm.
  diameter
81:1294:265
Museum collection

206.
UNIDENTIFIED PHOTOGRAPHER
[Eastman Kodak Company]
ca. 1890s
Gelatin silver print
Kodak #5 snapshot, 16.9 x 11.2
  cm.
79:2951:2
Museum collection

207.
UNIDENTIFIED PHOTOGRAPHER
[Girl and fence]
ca. 1890s
Gelatin silver print
Kodak # 1 snapshot, 6.3 cm.
  diameter
81:1154:4
Ex-collection of Alden Scott Boyer

208.
UNIDENTIFIED PHOTOGRAPHER
[Group portrait]
ca. 1890s
Gelatin silver print
Kodak # 1 snapshot, 6.3 cm.
  diameter
74:0245:52
Gift of Mrs. Raymond Albright

209.
UNIDENTIFIED PHOTOGRAPHER
[Group on tennis court]
ca. 1890s
Gelatin silver print
Kodak # 2 snapshot, 9.2 cm.
  diameter
81:2167:172
Gift of George B. Dryden

210.
UNIDENTIFIED PHOTOGRAPHER
[Interior scene]
ca. 1890s
Gelatin silver print
Kodak # 1 snapshot, 6.3 cm.
  diameter
74:0245:19
Gift of Mrs. Raymond Albright

211.
UNIDENTIFIED PHOTOGRAPHER
[Lifeboats]
ca. 1890s
Gelatin silver print
Kodak # 1 snapshot, 6.4 cm.
  diameter
81:1094:9
Gift of John Sears Wright

212.
UNIDENTIFIED PHOTOGRAPHER
[Unidentified architectural view]
ca. 1890s
Gelatin silver print
Kodak # 1 snapshot, 6.4 cm.
  diameter
81:1094:42
Gift of John Sears Wright

213.
UNIDENTIFIED PHOTOGRAPHER
[Unidentified boy in front of porch]
ca. 1890s
Gelatin silver print
Kodak # 2 snapshot, 9.2 cm.
  diameter
81:1684:156
Gift of Lyndon Wells

214.
UNIDENTIFIED PHOTOGRAPHER
[Unidentified group of women and
  children with watermelon]
ca. 1890s
Gelatin silver print
Kodak # 2 snapshot, 8.9 cm.
  diameter
81:2862:95
Museum collection

215.
UNIDENTIFIED PHOTOGRAPHER
[Unidentified infant in carriage]
ca. 1890s
Gelatin silver print
Kodak # 2 snapshot, 9.0 cm.
  diameter
81:2862:91
Museum collection

216.
UNIDENTIFIED PHOTOGRAPHER
[Unidentified landscape]
ca. 1890s
Gelatin silver print
Kodak # 1 snapshot, 6.4 cm.
  diameter
74:0245:51
Gift of Mrs. Raymond Albright

217.
UNIDENTIFIED PHOTOGRAPHER
[Unidentified landscape]
ca. 1890s
Gelatin silver print
Kodak # 1 snapshot, 6.3 cm.
  diameter
74:0245:55
Gift of Mrs. Raymond Albright

218.
UNIDENTIFIED PHOTOGRAPHER
[Unidentified male]
ca. 1890s
Gelatin silver print
Kodak # 2 snapshot, 9.2 cm.
  diameter
79:4186:17
Gift of Dr. & Mrs. Watson

219.
UNIDENTIFIED PHOTOGRAPHER
[Unidentified man on ship board]
ca. 1890s
Gelatin silver print
Kodak # 4 snapshot, 11.9 x 9.4
  cm.
82:3133:2
Gift of Mrs. Lyndon Wells

220.
UNIDENTIFIED PHOTOGRAPHER
[Unidentified men posing in front
  of house]
ca. 1890s
Gelatin silver print
Kodak #5 snapshot, 11.3 x 16.6
  cm.
82:1848:2
Museum collection

221.
UNIDENTIFIED PHOTOGRAPHER
[Unidentified men with walking
  sticks]
ca. 1890s
Gelatin silver print
Kodak # 2 snapshot, 9.2 cm.
  diameter
81:2603:97
Gift of Greene County Historical
  Society

222.
UNIDENTIFIED PHOTOGRAPHER
[Unidentified sculpture]
ca. 1890s
Gelatin silver print
Kodak # 1 snapshot, 6.4 cm.
  diameter
74:0245:7
Gift of Mrs. Raymond Albright

223.
E. H. DENIO
(active 1890s)
"Florence Bigallo"
ca. 1895
Gelatin silver print
Kodak # 3 snapshot, 7.6 x 10.0
  cm.
82:0085:29
Museum collection

224.
*EASTMAN KODAK COMPANY
(active 1881–)
Demostrator's catechism.
Rochester, Eastman Kodak
Company.
1897
Book, 41 pages
22.1 x 14.3 cm.
83:2020:1
Museum collection*

225.
*EASTMAN KODAK COMPANY
(active 1881–)
If you want it—Take it with a
Kodak/If it isn't an Eastman,
It isn't a Kodak
1900
Lithographic print
38.1 x 27.0 cm.
83:2015:11
Museum purchase*

226.
*EASTMAN KODAK COMPANY
(active 1881–)
Les "Brownie" Kodaks
ca. 1900
Lithographic print
29.5 x 39.2 cm.
73:0050:1
Museum collection*

227.
*C. IRVING FISHER
(active ca. 1900)
[Unidentified male]
ca. 1900
Gelatin silver print
11.2 x 9.2 cm.
82:1867:8
Gift of William McCann*

228.
*UNIDENTIFIED PHOTOGRAPHER
[Group portrait]
ca. 1900
Gelatin silver print
13.7 x 8.1 cm.
80:0346:13
Gift of Peter Geib*

229.
*UNIDENTIFIED PHOTOGRAPHER
[House]
1901
Gelatin silver print
5.8 x 10.4 cm.
79:4240:15
Gift of Allen Art Museum*

230.
*UNIDENTIFIED PHOTOGRAPHER
"Just a 1 lb. Bass, Ahmic Lake"
1908
Gelatin silver print
8.3 x 8.3 cm.
82:1854:2
Museum collection*

231.
*ROCHESTER NEWS CO.,
publisher
General Offices, Eastman Kodak
Co.
ca. 1910
Photomechanical reproduction
Post card, 7.9 x 12.9 cm.
81:9971:1
Gift of Dr. Fritz Wentzel*

232.
*UNIDENTIFIED PHOTOGRAPHER
[Woman in canoe]
ca. 1910
Gelatin silver print
8.2 x 8.2 cm.
82:1854:141
Museum collection*

233.
*EASTMAN KODAK COMPANY
(active 1881–)
Dope Mixing Barrels, Kodak Park
1911
from: Kodak Souvenir, December
4th, 1911
Gelatin silver print
24.0 x 18.8 cm.
83:2019:13
Museum collection*

234.
*EASTMAN KODAK COMPANY
(active 1881–)
Executive Offices
1911
from: Kodak Souvenir, December
4th, 1911
Gelatin silver print
19.0 x 24.0 cm.
83:2019:3
Museum collection*

235.
*EASTMAN KODAK COMPANY
(active 1881–)
[George Eastman and employees,
group portrait]
1911
from: Kodak Souvenir, December
4th, 1911
Gelatin silver print
16.3 x 21.5 cm.
83:2019:1
Museum collection*

236.
*EASTMAN KODAK COMPANY
(active 1881–)
Paper Box Department, Kodak
Park
1911
from: Kodak Souvenir, December
4th, 1911
Gelatin silver print
19.0 x 24.0 cm.
83:2019:16
Museum collection*

237.
*EASTMAN KODAK COMPANY
(active 1881–)
Paper Stock Room, Kodak Park
1911
from: Kodak Souvenir, December
4th, 1911
Gelatin silver print
24.0 x 18.9 cm.
83:2019:15
Museum collection*

238.
*EASTMAN KODAK COMPANY
(active 1881–)
Smoke Stacks, Kodak Park, 366
ft. high
1911
from: Kodak Souvenir, December
4th, 1911
Gelatin silver print
21.5 x 10.7 cm.
83:2019:8
Museum collection*

239.
*EASTMAN KODAK COMPANY
(active 1881–)
Take a Kodak with you
ca. 1912
Lithographic print
72.8 x 47.2 cm.
76:0232:166
Museum purchase*

240.
*UNIDENTIFIED PHOTOGRAPHER
"Auto tours-New York to
Massachusetts, Maine to Cape
Cod"
1913
Gelatin silver print
9.3 x 11.0 cm.
82:1867:16
Gift of William McCann*

241.
*UNIDENTIFIED PHOTOGRAPHER
"Auto tours-New York to
Massachusetts, Maine to Cape
Cod"
1913
Gelatin silver print
11.2 x 9.2 cm.
82:1867:22
Gift of William McCann*

242.
*EASTMAN KODAK COMPANY
(active 1881–)
"Kodak, the Growth and Triumph
of an Idea"
ca. 1920s
Lithographic print
18.0 x 12.3 cm.
L83:2322:1
Lent by a private collection*

243.
*FRED MAYER
(active 1920s)
"Eight selected Kodak pictures of
Columbia River Highway
Oregon"
ca. 1920s
Gelatin silver print
10.3 x 5.7 cm., each
82:2485:9-16
Gift of 3M Co., ex-collection Louis
Walton Sipley*

244.
*FRED MAYER
(active 1920s)
"Eight selected Kodak pictures of
the Hood Loop Oregon"
ca. 1920s
Gelatin silver print
10.3 x 5.7 cm., each
82:2485:1-8
Gift of 3M Co., ex-collection Louis
Walton Sipley*

245.
*UNIDENTIFIED PHOTOGRAPHER
[Dog with gramophone]
ca. 1920
Gelatin silver print
7.9 x 7.6 cm.
82:1854:17
Museum collection*

246.
*EASTMAN KODAK COMPANY
(active 1881–)
[Woman with dog]
ca. 1925
Gelatin silver print
31.8 x 20.3 cm.
83:2017:3
Museum purchase*

247.
*EASTMAN KODAK COMPANY
(active 1881–)
Kodak as you go
ca. 1932
Photomechanical reproduction
38.2 x 34.9 cm.
83:2017:2
Museum purchase*

248.
*ROCHESTER NEWS CO.,
publisher
Aerial View of Kodak Park Works,
Eastman Kodak Company
ca. 1940s
Photomechanical reproduction
Post card, 7.9 x 13.0 cm.
81:9971:3
Gift of Dr. Fritz Wentzel*

BAUSCH & LOMB OPTICAL CO.
ROCHESTER, NEW YORK

249.
BAUSCH & LOMB PORTRAIT
 LENS
ca. 1890
84:083:5
Gift of Bausch & Lomb

250.
UNICUM SHUTTER
1897
84:084:07
Museum collection

251.
SIGMAR PORTRAIT LENS,
 16 INCH F/4
1929
84:083:2
Museum collection

252.
CINEMASCOPE
 ANAMORPHOSER
1952
84:082:01-02
Gift of Elliot Press

F. A. BROWNELL
ROCHESTER, NEW YORK

253.
BROWNELL STEREO CAMERA
ca. 1883
L84:107:1
Loaned by Frank Brownell
 Mehlenbacher

CENTURY CAMERA CO.
ROCHESTER, NEW YORK

254.
CENTURY CAMERA, MODEL 46,
 5x7 INCH
1905
74:037:1699
Museum collection

D. O. INDUSTRIES
ROCHESTER, NEW YORK

255.
6"–9" GOLDEN NAVITAR
 PROJECTION LENS
1979
L:84:079:1
Loaned by D. O. Industries

256.
48 INCH LASER SCAN
 OBJECTIVE LENS
1981
L:84:079:5
Loaned by D. O. Industries

257.
420–860mm ZOOM SCAN LENS
1982
L:84:079:4
Loaned by D. O. Industries

258.
LASER DIODE COLLIMATING
 LENS
ca. 1984
L:84:079:6
Loaned by D. O. Industries

EASTMAN DRY PLATE
& FILM CO.
ROCHESTER, NEW YORK

259.
THE KODAK CAMERA
1888
77:085:8
Museum collection

EASTMAN KODAK CO.—
FOLMER & SCHWING
DIVISION
ROCHESTER, NEW YORK

260.
POCKET KODAK STYLE 1
1895
74:037:1507
Gift of Eastman Kodak Patent
 Museum

261.
#1A FOLDING POCKET KODAK
1899
74:037:1297
Gift of Mr. L. A. Rew

262.
PANORAM #4
1899
74:037:1504
Museum collection

263.
#1 BROWNIE
1900
74:037:1107
Gift of Mr. J. R. Miller

264.
RB 4x5 GRAFLEX
ca. 1902
74:037:2423
Gift of Graflex, Inc.

265.
#10 CIRKUT CAMERA
ca. 1905
78:1373:4
Gift of Graflex, Inc.

266.
3A GRAFLEX
1907
74:037:2412
Museum collection

267.
VEST POCKET KODAK
1912
74:037:1961
Museum collection

268.
4x5 SPEED GRAPHIC
1912
74:037:2427
Gift of Graflex, Inc.

269.
CINE KODAK 16—MODEL A
1923
78:191:86
Museum collection

270.
CINE KODAK SPECIAL
1933
81:2793:1
Gift of Mrs. Q. Treuthart

271.
CINE KODAK EIGHT—MODEL 25
1933
81:2333:3
Gift of Peter Geib

272.
3A FOLDING POCKET KODAK
ca. 1935
74:037:2874
Museum collection

273.
KODAK BANTAM SPECIAL
1936
L:83:865:1
Museum collection

274.
SUPERMATIC SHUTTER #2
1940
84:084:05
Museum collection

275.
KODAK EKTRA
1941
74:015:36, 83:0626:661
Museum collection

276.
CAROUSEL 550 SLIDE
 PROJECTOR
1961
81:2536:22
Museum collection

277.
INSTAMATIC 100
1963
74:037:246
Gift of Eastman Kodak Company

278.
KODAK POCKET INSTAMATIC 20
1972
74:028:3049
Gift of Eastman Kodak Company

279.
KODAK DISC 4000 CAMERA
1982
82:1002:3, 84:085:17
Gift of Eastman Kodak Company

ELGEET OPTICAL COMPANY
ROCHESTER, NEW YORK

280.
CINE-TEL LENS
3 inch focal length, f/2.9
ca. 1950
L84:079:3
Loaned by D. O. Industries

281.
OPTO-NAVITAR TELEPHOTO
 LENS
38mm focal length, f/1.8
ca. 1950
L84:079:2
Loaned by D. O. Industries

GCA CORPORATION,
TROPEL DIVISION
FAIRPORT, NEW YORK

282.
LASER DISC RECORDING LENS
Numerical aperture 0.66
Focal length 3.6mm, Weight 4.1
 grams
1983
L84:086:2
Loaned by GCA Corporation,
 Tropel Division

**GRAFLEX INC.
ROCHESTER, NEW YORK**

283.
COMBAT GRAPHIC 70
1952
81:2813:2
Museum collection

284.
GRAFLEX XL
1966
80:193:1
Gift of Graflex Inc.

**GUNDLACH OPTICAL CO.
ROCHESTER, NEW YORK**

285.
KORONA CAMERA SERIES 1A,
   4x5 INCH
ca. 1900
77:552:446
Museum collection

286.
RADAR ANASTIGMAT
ca. 1924
68:427
Museum collection

**ILEX OPTICAL CO.
ROCHESTER, NEW YORK**

287.
ILEX PARAGON TELEPHOTO
ca. 1940
76:016:14
Museum collection

288.
#5 UNIVERSAL SYNCHRO
   SHUTTER
1945
84:084:08
Museum collection

289.
ANASTIGMAT LENS, IN #3
   UNIVERSAL SHUTTER, 3 INCH
   F/119
ca. 1950
84:084:06
Museum collection

**MONROE CAMERA CO.
ROCHESTER, NEW YORK**

290.
SMALL TONGS CAMERA,
   2x2 ¼ INCH
1897
74:037:1553
Museum collection

**MOVETTE, INC.
ROCHESTER, NEW YORK**

291.
MOVETTE SYSTEM
1914
80:043:7
Gift of The Strong Museum

**PROJECTION OPTICS CO.,
INC.
ROCHESTER, NEW YORK**

292.
#2 PROJEX MOTION PICTURE
   PROJECTION LENS, 4 INCH
   FOCUS
ca. 1940
84:083:1
Museum collection

**RAY CAMERA CO.
ROCHESTER, NEW YORK**

293.
RAY NO. 7 CAMERA, 5x7 INCH
1900
74:37:1733
Museum collection

**REICHENBACH, MOREY
AND WILL
ROCHESTER, NEW YORK**

294.
ALTA C—5x7 PLATE CAMERA
1898
68:258
Museum collection

**ROCHESTER CAMERA CO.
ROCHESTER, NEW YORK**

295.
FOLDING GEM POCO CAMERA
1898
74:037:1525
Museum collection

**ROCHESTER CAMERA AND
SUPPLY CO.
ROCHESTER, NEW YORK**

296.
TELEPHOTO CYCLE PREMO
   CAMERA, 4x5 INCH
1898
74:037:2515
Museum collection

**ROCHESTER OPTICAL CO.
ROCHESTER, NEW YORK**

297.
PREMO LONG FOCUS CAMERA,
   5x7 INCH
1902
68:285
Museum collection

298.
LONG FOCUS PREMO
ca. 1905
74:037:1923
Museum collection

**SENECA CAMERA CO.
ROCHESTER, NEW YORK**

299.
SENECA VIEW CAMERA, 8x10
   INCH
1903
77:849:194
Museum collection

300.
SENCO #1 ROLEFILM CAMERA,
   2 ¼ x3 ¼ inch
1912
74:037:1662
Gift of Mr. Y. H. Votypka

**SUNART PHOTO CO.
ROCHESTER, NEW YORK**

301.
MAGAZINE CAMERA, 4x5 INCH
1899
80:043:3
Museum collection

**TROPEL, INC.
FAIRPORT, NEW YORK**

302.
REOGON AERIAL CAMERA
   LENS
90 degree field at f/2.5
1968
L84:086:3
Loaned by GCA Corporation,
   Tropel Division

303.
MICROTROPAR LENS, F/1.9
1972
L84:086:1
Loaned by GCA Corporation,
   Tropel Division

**WM. H. WALKER & CO.
ROCHESTER, NEW YORK**

304.
WALKER'S POCKET CAMERA
1881
74:037:1584
Gift of Eastman Kodak Patent
   Museum

**WOLLENSAK OPTICAL CO.
ROCHESTER, NEW YORK**

305.
#2 OPTIMO SHUTTER
1909
84:084:03
Museum collection

306.
BEACH MULTIFOCAL LENS,
   SERIES A, 14 INCH FOCAL
   LENGTH
1935
84:083:04
Museum collection

307.
GRAPHEX SHUTTER
ca. 1950
84:084:04
Museum collection

LIST OF LENDERS

Douglas Beube
Marilyn Bridges
Tim Callahan
Guenther Cartwright
D.O. Industries
Eastman Kodak Company
GCA Corp., Tropel Division
Bruce Horowitz
Ted Kawalerski
Leslie Kippen
Frank Mehlenbacher
Louis Ouzer
Charlotte Quehl
Richard M. Rowe
Jane Alden Stevens
Joseph Vitone
Andrew D. Wolfe
Del Zogg

ACKNOWLEDGEMENTS

Any exhibition of this size and complexity owes much to a great number of people, without whose efforts and goodwill the project could not have been realized.

On the staff of this Museum, especial thanks are extended to Print Archivist David Wooters, Curatorial Assistants Heather Alberts, Joanne Lukitsh and Morgan Wesson, and former Curatorial Assistant Bonnie Ford, who was initially responsible for surveying the collection's holdings of Rochester photography. Librarians Rachel Stuhlman, Betty Seidel, Gail McClain, and Norma Feld; Volunteer Karen Chase and Intern Stephen Dingler; Grant Romer, Sergio Burgi, Elizabeth Frey, and Constance McCabe of the Conservation Department; Rick Hock, James Via and Carolyn Zaft of the Exhibitions Department; Registrars Ann McCabe and James Conlin; Linda McCausland and Barbara Puorro Galasso of Print Services; Mike Hager, Negative Archivist and Christine Hawrylak of the Public Relations Office, are also to be thanked. Senior cataloguer Del Zogg was of immeasureable aid in assisting with the computer cataloguing of the checklist, as was the Director of Interdepartmental Services, Andrew Eskind. Former Director of Development Dan Meyers and Museum Director Robert Mayer encouraged and supported this project from the start.

Several people from the Rochester community were of special assistance to this exhibition: Dr. Walter Clark, Nick Graver, Leatrice Kemp of the Rochester Museum and Science Center, Dr. Rudolf Kingslake, Mrs. Roberta LaChiusa of the Susan B. Anthony House, Nathan Lyons and the staff of the Visual Studies Workshop, Robert Meyer and Julia Wyant of Robert Meyer Design, Robert Navias, Charlotte Quehl, Dick Rowe of Rowe Professional Photographers, Inc., and Mary Smith of Hamlin. Additional thanks are due Eastman Kodak Company and, in particular, Darlene Aiken, Lois Gauch, Michael More and Marge Petschke. Gratitude is also extended to Andrew Wolfe of Wolfe Publications for providing important information.

The Museum would also like to express its appreciation for all assistance provided by the Rochester Sesquicentennial Committee for its grant towards the implementation of the exhibition and to D. O. Industries of East Rochester, which also provided funds for the installation of the exhibitions.

Lastly, very sincere thanks are due all photographers of Rochester whose creative and talented work contributed vastly to the pleasure of putting this exhibition together. The preponderance of exceptional photography available for selection and display far exceeded the show's physical limitations; in no way should exclusion be considered criticism.

R.A.S.
J.P.
P.L.C.

ADDITIONAL READINGS

Ackerman, Carl. George Eastman. *Boston: Houghton Mifflin, 1930.*

Brayer, Betsy. "Mr. Eastman Builds a House." Brighton-Pittsford Post *series, 1979-1980.*

Coe, Brian. George Eastman and the Early Photographers. *London: Priory Press, 1973.*

Coe, Brian and Gates, Paul. The Snapshot Photograph, The Rise of Popular Photography, 1888-1939. *London: Ash and Grant, 1977.*

Fordyce, Robert Penn. Stereo Photography in Rochester, New York up to 1900. *Rochester, New York, 1975.*

Hosmer, Howard. Monroe County (1821-1971). *Rochester, New York; Rochester Museum and Science Center, 1971.*

Jenkins, Reese. Images and Enterprise, Technology and the American Photographic Industry 1839-1925. *Baltimore: Johns Hopkins University Press, 1975.*

Kingslake, Rudolf. The Rochester Camera and Lens Companies. *Rochester, The Photographic Historical Society, 1974.*

McKelvey, Blake. A Panoramic History of Rochester and Monroe County New York. *Woodland Hills, California: Windsor Publications; 1979.*

Mehlenbacher, Frank B. "Frank A. Brownell: Mr. Eastman's Camera Maker." Image, *June 1983., Volume 26, No. 2.*

Newhall, Beaumont. The Daguerreotype in America. *New York: Dover, 1975.*

Smith, Mary E. Behind the Lens: Nineteenth Century and Turn-of-the-Century Photographers of Western Monroe County, New York. *Rochester, New York: Monroe County Photo-History Project, 1980.*

Taft, Robert. Photography and the American Scene, A Social History 1839-1889. *New York: Dover, 1938.*

Wolfe, Andrew D. Creative Change for the University of Rochester and Its Community. *Rochester, New York: University of Rochester, 1953.*

Wolfe, Andrew D. Views of Old Rochester and the Genesee Country from Indian Days to 1918. *Pittsford, New York: Phoenix Press, 1970.*